D1112247

KILL THE COWBOY

KILL  COWBOY

A Battle of Mythology in the New West

SHARMAN APT RUSSELL

Addison-Wesley Publishing Company

Reading, Massachusetts   Menlo Park, California   New York
Don Mills, Ontario   Wokingham, England   Amsterdam   Bonn
Sydney   Singapore   Tokyo   Madrid   San Juan
Paris   Seoul   Milan   Mexico City   Taipei

The poem "Heaven" by Dick Hays on pages 151–152 is from the book *From a Cowboy's Point of View*. Reprinted by permission of Marie Hays.

Many of the designations used by manufacturers and sellers to distinguish their products are claimed as trademarks. Where those designations appear in this book and Addison-Wesley was aware of a trademark claim, the designations have been printed in initial capital letters (e.g., Styrofoam).

Library of Congress Cataloging-in-Publication Data
Russell, Sharman Apt.
    Kill the cowboy : a battle of mythology in the new West   /
Sharman Apt Russell.
        p.   cm.
    Includes bibliographical references and index.
    ISBN 0-201-58123-X
    1. Man—Influence on nature—West (U.S.)   2. Cow-
boys—West (U.S.)—Attitudes.   3. Ranchers—West (U.S.)—
Attitudes.   4. Prairie ecology—West (U.S.)   5. Soil
degradation—West (U.S.)   6. Range management—West
(U.S.)   7. Range policy—West (U.S.)   I. Title.
GF504.W35R87   1993
333.74'0978—dc20   93-525
                                                                CIP

Jacket design by Wendell Minor
Text design by Linda Koegel
Set in 10-point Bembo by Carol Woolverton

1 2 3 4 5 6 7 8 9-MU-96959493
First printing, May 1993

For Peter

CONTENTS

Author's Note   *xiii*

1. *Kill the Cowboy*   1

2. *The Public-Lands Debate*   14

3. *The Physics of Beauty*   74

4. *The Green Woman*   148

5. *Epilogue*   194

Selected Bibliography and Notes   199

Index   211

AUTHOR'S NOTE

THIS BOOK offers no simple answer. Instead, I have chosen to juxtapose a number of different viewpoints. I am mainly concerned with issues of land health and wildlife in the American West. When I use the term *environmentalist,* I am referring to people who sympathize with or belong to groups such as the Sierra Club, National Wildlife Federation, Wilderness Society, and Nature Conservancy. Very recently a new political administration has asked some of these environmentalists to help manage millions of acres of public land in the West. Changes are coming quickly. We can all hear the sound of that train. In the next month—in the next week—there will be adjustments in grazing fee costs, for example, or in how grazing allotments are managed. I believe such change is necessary. I also know that the polarization of groups struggling to determine land use in the West is only going to increase, perhaps for many years to come.

Many people helped me in this project. I must particularly thank those who allowed themselves to be interviewed and profiled. I also thank my husband, Peter Russell, for his constant and faithful support.

KILL THE COWBOY

1. KILL THE COWBOY

> 66 *The meaning of America still resides, somehow, in the West. From the beginning it is clear that the spaces west of where you are always seem to contain the essence of America.* 99
> —Frederick Turner

> 66 *By myth I mean the world view or imagistic lens through which a people conceive and perceive the data of experience.* 99
> —Jay McDaniel

WE TAKE A cup of coffee and move into the backyard. Perhaps we live in a city or town. Houses surround our house. We listen to the noises of other people: children not our own, pet dogs barking, the ubiquitous hum of cars. Our eyes seek the rim of distant mountains. They are volcanic, rugged, and bare boned, gentled only with distance. Something in us flies out to them, subtle and fast, and something returns. For the rest of the day, we may not think of these mountains again. Still, we will seek them out tomorrow or the next day or the next. Something in us will fly out to them, and something will return.

Wherever we live, whoever we are, we respond to landscape. In-

I

articulate, slumbering, distilled into myth and image, the connections are there. The roots are historic and archetypic. We water a houseplant because a farmer lives inside us. We drive a coastal highway, and the sailor begins to sing. We take a walk; the explorer charts the course. We feel fearful when the mountains are too high or the plain too big. We can feel liberated for the same reasons or for very different ones. Sometimes we admire land as we admire a painting, moved by the beauty of shape and color. Often, we desire to enter that painting. We want to buy some of this land! We want to live in it! Myths gather in quickly now. Images resonate. We seek, as human beings, to find our place in the natural world.

Here in the West, the dominant myth—of course—is the cowboy. Our love for cowboys, in the strict definition of the word, has little to do with reality. So few Americans want the lonely job of herding cattle or sheep at $800 a month, plus room and board, that foreign workers are hired to fill the shortage. When the term *cowboy*, however, is extended to include ranchers and the support system of ranchers—men and women who own feed stores, shoe horses, sell agricultural equipment, truck animals, own a steer or two, and "cowboy" on the weekend—then it embraces a lifestyle quite real in the small towns and countrysides of half the United States. Cowboys are the icon of the rural West. They have much to do with how all Americans think about the West. They have much to do with our cultural dreams of freedom and solitude, of riding a horse across golden fields as thunderclouds roil across the sky, of sleeping peacefully under the arc of the Milky Way, of waking alone to the bitter light of dawn. In these dreams, we test ourselves on the anvil of self-sufficiency. In these dreams, we know the grandeur of an untrammeled continent. We are intimate with animals. We are intimate with the earth.

Real ranchers and cowboys touch such heights every day. They do not analyze their connection to the land or, for that matter, to their own animal body. These connections are part of their daily routine.

They have found a way to enter the extreme beauty and daunting open spaces of the American West: they work in it.

In the course of this job, they see sunrises, mud puddles, hoarfrost, willows, aspens, junipers, pines, rimrock, slickrock, ponds, stream banks, meadows, gullies, sunsets, and stars. They touch horsehair, cowhide, horns, bones, wounds, rope, and fence posts. Centaurlike, they can run twenty miles an hour, cover thirty miles a day, and have a great view all the while. They are physically alert and competent because they must be. They learn to endure. They live with their own company. They feel at home in the dark.

There are those who would argue that we need the cowboy now more than ever. We need every man, woman, and child who has found a way to slip into the land that rolls past our car windows. As our last frontier urbanizes, we need the psychic ballast of people who make their livelihood directly from soil, grass, and water. We need people who understand, rather more than the rest of us, that our society—our houses, VCRs, cereal boxes—depends on a base of natural resources. We need cultural diversity. We need dreams.

Thirty years ago, that might have been a concluding sentence.

Today there is much more to say about the cowboy. Dreams, as we discover again and again, are half seduction. And the cowboy, the se- ductive cowboy, has a dark side.

For a growing number of critics, the cowboy's connection to the land is clearly skewed—in favor of production. Over 70 percent of the West is grazed. To the cowboy, this is good, for the land must be used. You can't eat scenery. Although he or she would not admit it, the cowboy's job is to transform the wild West into something that resembles, prosaically, a feedlot.

Thus, wild animals become competition. Predators such as bears, coyotes, mountain lions, wolves, and eagles must be destroyed. Elk eat the grass meant for cows. The tunnels of prairie dogs trip livestock.

Cowboys are intimate with wildlife in the sense that they must control its activity and growth. They are intimate with the horses they break and castrate. They are intimate with the cows they protect in order to market. They are intimate with the land they seek to tame. Theirs—critics say—is the intimacy of oppression.

It began in the late nineteenth century, when huge herds of cattle roamed the "sea of grass" from Texas to Montana. Rangeland can be defined as those places considered unsuitable for intensive cultivation or forestry. They often are dry, rough, extremely cold or extremely hot, with poor drainage and shallow soil. Such lands make up about half the United States. In many areas they were originally covered with lush stands of perennial grass. The use of this resource, "dried hay on the stem," was so easy. It was so profitable. Who could resist the combination?

In fact, most rangeland did evolve and coexist with grazing animals and can support a moderate livestock industry. Moderation, however, was never the western way. And "forage fever" swept the nation as surely as the enthusiasm for gold. In 1884, a Colorado livestock journal declared, "Untold millions in Europe and America are ready to invest in range cattle, and cattle is one of those investments men cannot pay too much for, since if left alone, they will multiply, replenish, and grow out of a bad bargain."

Cattle and cattle companies did multiply. The 1870 estimate of four million to five million cows on the western range peaked at thirty-five million to forty million fourteen years later. Sheep also increased dramatically. In some areas, the explosion of domestic livestock coincided with years of drought. Massive die-offs became common in the 1880s and 1890s; rotting carcasses were so thick that a man could throw rocks from one dead animal to the next. By 1912, the former head of the Grazing Section of the early Forest Service would look back and write: "The grazing lands were stocked far beyond their capacity; vegetation was cropped by hungry animals before it had an opportunity to reproduce; valuable forage plants gave way to worthless weeds, and the productive capacity of the land rapidly diminished."

The West is still recovering from its own history. Some places will never recover. Today, the health of our rangeland is unclear. The Forest Service in the U.S. Department of Agriculture and the Bureau of Land Management in the U.S. Department of the Interior admit that they don't have information for a quarter of the public land they lease grazing rights on; they estimate that another half could be rated as fair or poor, the lower two of four categories. Groups such as the National Wildlife Federation believe these figures to be conservative; ranchers believe they are an exaggeration. A 1992 report to the United Nations Conference on Environment and Development estimated that half of the U.S. rangeland (both public and private) is severely degraded, with its carrying capacity reduced by at least 50 percent. Of greatest concern are the riparian areas, those narrow habitats around streams and rivers. Stream-lying areas make up only a fraction of the West, but they are crucial to its ecology and to the survival of wildlife.

On the positive side, most people agree that the uplands have improved steadily over the last five decades. Overall, the American range is healthier now than it has been in one hundred years.

What sustained heavy grazing has done, here in this country and all over the world, is contribute to the insidious drying of our planet, a premature grief like mortal illness in a child. Globally, half of the earth's solid ground is grazed by some domestic animal. In the United States, that animal is usually a cow raised for beef or dairy products. Throughout Asia and Africa, however, livestock also plow the majority of agricultural land, carry goods to market, provide clothing and fuel, produce fertilizer, and serve as the poor man's bank account. Internationally, the number of domestic grazers has soared, mainly because of a demand for more meat.

Briefly, when cattle overgraze perennial native grasses in the American West, they allow annual weeds and tough shrubs such as cheatgrass, tumbleweed, sage, and mesquite to spread. This shift in species is the major form of range degradation. The new plants are less efficient in anchoring topsoil and leave the ground vulnerable to trampling hooves and erosion. Without the perennial grasses, the fires that naturally control the spread of shrubs lose their tinder. Human suppression of fire also has contributed to the dramatic increase of brush such as juniper and creosote. As the variety of plant species declines, so does the variety of wildlife. At the same time, there is simply less forage for everyone. Under continued overgrazing, bare ground becomes compacted and rainwater rushes over the surface, carrying away more soil and turning streambeds into dry gullies. Water tables fall for lack of replenishment. Flooding occurs more frequently. Sediment clogs waterways, dams, and estuaries.

Water itself is a problem. Cows need ten to fifteen gallons of it every day. The West is mythically "cattle country." Yet it commonly requires one hundred or more acres in the arid Southwest to support one cow; it takes one acre in Georgia. With modern technology, water can always be found, diverted, and used, but the cost is high. On the range, cows trample and abuse the fragile stream areas. Beef feedlots rely on crops raised with water pumped up from depleted aquifers such as the Ogallala. In many states, livestock agriculture consumes one-third of an irrigation system linked to salinization of the soil.

All of this, all the efforts of the eleven major western states, produces only 20 percent of the country's beef. The public lands provide only 7 percent of the total forage and 2 percent of the total feed (forage, hay, and grain) consumed by beef cattle in the contiguous United States. (Although sheep also graze on public land, cattle consume the vast amount of grass.)

It sounds awful.

Yet a description of how farming in the Midwest has affected that ecosystem would be just as horrendous. The construction of cities and towns completely obliterates a natural habitat. Almost any large-scale effort by humans is destructive, as is the lifestyle of almost every

American. Our problem is how to minimize this destruction and still get the natural resources we want and need. No one seriously suggests that we stop being destructive altogether—stop growing corn or stop building houses.

But more and more people *are* questioning the grazing of cattle in the West. Suddenly, it is not the cowboy on the open plain who is so seductive, it is the open plain itself. We want not the Marlboro man but what he stands in front of.

The heart of this controversy lies in that half of the West that belongs to the American public. Many environmentalists have made the health of this rangeland a priority, and a new range war is being fought—in every national forest and on every piece of Bureau of Land Management (BLM) land, in every western town, and in every western city.

At a Montana county fair, a red wagon is filled with manure and topped with signs that read "U.S. Forest Service" and "National Wildlife Federation." The Arizona Cattleman's Association lobbies to kill thousands of elk in the national forest. An editorial in a Denver newspaper skewers "welfare ranchers" and condemns the cow as an "alien species." A woman working to end a government predator-control program gets a death threat. So does the man who runs such a program. Somewhere in Nevada, a rancher finds Coke poured into the engine of his tractor. Somewhere in New Mexico, an environmentalist's dog is shot and skinned like a coyote.

Much is at stake. We are talking about a lot of land.

In sixteen of the western states, we lease to ranchers some 307 million acres, an area the size of the eastern seaboard, from Maine to Florida. Nearly 80 percent of the land managed by the Forest Service and BLM is grazed. About half of designated wilderness areas are grazed. A quarter of our national parks, national monuments, national recreation areas, national memorials, and historic parks are grazed. Thirty-five percent of our national wildlife refuges are grazed.

Such a program, obviously, requires management. The government uses a system of over 30,000 grazing allotments which vary in size from forty acres to over one million. About 23,600 permittees lease grazing privileges on this federal land, for which they pay a specific fee. They are expected to follow certain rules. On each allotment, Forest Service rangers or BLM range conservationists determine a plan—how many cows there can be, when these cows can be there, and where these cows can go.

Grazing on public land is an administrative mandate. Allotments are grazed to the full extent that the area can support livestock. Eventually, a rancher will lose a lease if he or she does not use it. Politically and practically, it has been very difficult to retire an allotment—even for ecological reasons. This concept is rooted in history. The U.S. government first intended to give away or sell to its citizens almost all of the territory acquired through conquest and Manifest Destiny. Later, some of this land was protected or put in reserve as a continual source of natural resources. These resources clearly were to remain available to local economies and entrepreneurs.

Through most of the twentieth century, most ranchers thought of their BLM or Forest Service allotment as a private kingdom. Typically, they had a small base of deeded property and then leased grazing rights on thousands of acres of federal land. This land often was remote, forgotten, and rarely visited. The rancher might have "inherited" the lease from his or her parents, who might have gotten it from their parents. (Grazing permits cannot really be owned but are tied, obscurely, to the base of private property. This relationship increases that property's value and that value, in turn, is taxed by the Internal Revenue Service. Banks also consider a grazing permit as collateral for a loan. In short, although grazing leases are not considered real property, they are treated as such.) After years of driving cattle through these valleys and hills, after a lifetime of knowing a place, daily, deeply, physically and emotionally, a rancher might well believe that the public land was no longer public.

On its part, the government did little to discourage that idea.

Now, there are fewer kingdoms in the world. There are more people and, of these, there are more who lust for some approximation of what ranchers have. On bad days, we all know that the earth is shrinking. The good things in life—air, water, beauty—are being gobbled up, and we must fight like children over the last pieces of candy. Environmentalists have important concerns about land health. But ranchers have historic claims they will not relinquish easily. From their perspective, the environmentalist is simply trying to muzzle in. In truth, land health is not *always* the issue. Sometimes non- ranchers just want to see elk instead of cows, camping sites instead of cowpies, views without fences. They want a piece of the action.

The numbers in this range war are deceptive.

Match 23,600 permittees with the National Wildlife Federation, which has a membership of over five million people. The Sierra Club has thirty times as many members as there are public-lands ranchers. The Wilderness Society has 390,000 members; the Nature Conservancy has 550,000. Across the West, too, local organizations are springing up like wildflowers after a good rain. These men and women see the public land as *their* backyard. They often have moved specifically to rural Oregon or Montana or Arizona because of a particular national forest or wilderness area.

It would seem that public-lands ranchers don't have a chance.

Yet the livestock industry remains an extremely powerful force in the West. Ranchers got here first, and wealthy ranchers often went into politics, as did their sons and grandsons. Many western governors, senators, and congressional representatives have ranches themselves. (If you have money in Wyoming, you don't buy beachfront property—you buy a ranch.) Cowboys, in any case, play well in Washington, D.C., where their dress is colorful and their authenticity valued.

Ranchers are also loyal. Public-lands ranchers make up only 3 percent of all livestock producers in the United States and 10 percent of those in the sixteen Western states. But ranchers stand behind their own. If ranching is not good enough for federal land—if we must protect the West from cows—then every rancher's image is tarnished.

The issue of range degradation, as well, is surprisingly complex and controversial. Wildlife biologist Allan Savory, for example, insists that "overresting" perennial grama grasses can cause more harm than overgrazing. He believes that land managed by environmental organizations is in worse shape than land grazed by cows, and his Center for Holistic Resource Management in Albuquerque is attended by hundreds of ranchers, BLM range conservationists, and Forest Service officials. It *is* true that without fire or the presence of some grazers (either wild or domestic), grass usually is replaced by brush. Some range studies in the Chihuahuan Desert suggest that light or moderate grazing by livestock can improve the long-term recovery of land as well as or better than no grazing. As usual, science is subjective. The research on range management is not a chorus of agreement.

Perhaps most important, the public-lands rancher's struggle to survive resonates for many westerners. Miners and loggers ally with the rancher. They, too, want traditional access to the resources of the public land. Popular groups such as "People for the West" advocate "wise use" policies of continued and intensive grazing, logging, and mining. Even private landowners fear that their rights will be eroded by new environmental regulations. There is strong and historic sentiment in the West against any form of interference—from resource managers or from environmentalists or from your next-door neighbor. There is a great resistance to change and a great desire for continuity.

Despite the growing polarization, I believe that an opportunity exists to find common ground, in all senses of that phrase. The public lands, after all, are not just a gift from our parents, an inheritance over which we can squabble and litigate. They are a gift to our children and to our grandchildren and to our great-grandchildren—even, as the Iroquois suggest, to the seventh generation to come.

These mountains are our watersheds. These trees produce oxygen. These gene pools are our future.

The conservationist Aldo Leopold wrote, "We abuse land because we regard it as a commodity, belonging to us. When we see land as a community to which we belong, we may begin to use it with love and respect."

Optimistically, our battle over the public lands could include this transition, from commodity to community.

Neither side can afford to be arrogant.

What *is* the purpose of a national forest? What will it be in a hundred years? What defines a wilderness area? What does the word *community* really mean?

We know much less than we thought we knew. We should be careful of knowing too much now.

The ranching lifestyle is a root growing deep into western soil. My own family has a marginal ranching history of which I am proud. My mother's grandparents came to Arizona from Texas at the turn of the century. My great-grandmother homesteaded in the Chiricahua Mountains. She lost her land during the Great Depression and later retreated into the hills to prospect a small mining claim. When he was young, my grandfather worked as a ranch hand up and down the Southwest. I have the requisite great-aunt who got married on horseback. None of this had much to do with cows. Ranching and mining and horsemanship were simply the ways my relatives knew to anchor themselves to the land. Although I grew up in Phoenix, I have chosen deliberately to live my life in rural New Mexico. When my husband and I came here to the Mimbres Valley, the first thing we did was buy twelve acres of waving grama grass, scrub oak, and alligator juniper. We also spent more than we could afford for the right to irrigate one acre from the Mimbres River. We, too, wanted to work the land. We wanted to be at home.

I have lived in the Mimbres Valley now for twelve years. Ninety

percent of the ranchers here have grazing permits on the nearby
Gila National Forest, Gila Wilderness, Aldo Leopold Wilderness, or
BLM land. Many of these ranches are small "heartbreak operations,"
run by people whose families came to New Mexico generations ago.

The older cowboys are a bitter breed. Their community is dissolving
as more ranchers fail to make a living and as more sons and daughters turn the family ranch into a subdivision. Their sense of place in
society is threatened. They have always felt proud of what they did
and of who they were. They have, in fact, even felt righteous. Now,
suddenly, they are the bad guys.

Here in this valley, there are more houses every day, more trailers,
a new grocery store, another gas station. People move here and commute to Silver City, thirty miles to the west. People retire here. Non-
country people like myself come to live in the country. Rather
quickly, the Mimbres is changing from a ranching community to a
kind of rural suburbia.

The conflicts between ranchers and environmentalists are very
real. Both sides feel fear and anger and a deep sense of loss. For those
of us who balance ecological concerns with our own desire to ride
a horse across a golden plain, the question is painfully immediate. If
we "kill the cowboy," who will replace him?

Out of our fear and anger, much is lost and not enough is gained
if we only find new laws and management plans. We need, as well,
new ways to live in the West. We need new myths and new role
models, ones that include heroines as well as heroes, urbanites as well
as country folk, ecologists as well as individualists. Ranchers need
these things as much as anyone if they are going to be ranching in
the twenty-first century.

"For a long time, I thought that being a cowboy was the wildest,
most wonderful life a person could lead," a neighbor once told me.
"But a cowboy has to dress a certain way. He has to talk a certain
way. He has to think a certain way. It's a dead end. Finally, I didn't
want to be that confined. I didn't want to be just what a cowboy is
supposed to be."

My own concerns are not entirely academic. My five-year-old son has identified himself as a cowboy ever since he could ride a rocking horse. He has played with innumerable herds of plastic animals and dreams of riding his pony in the hills behind our house. He believes that one day he will ride a larger horse, wear a six-shooter, and chase cows.

The bitter antagonism between environmentalists and ranchers is striking because in many ways they share the same needs and the same values. They are both seeking connection. They are both seeking ways to enter the landscape.

If there were no cowboys, my son would have to invent them.

Connection. Invention. Reinvention.

This may be the real work of the West.

2. THE PUBLIC-LANDS DEBATE

> *The teaching mythology we grew up with in the American West is a pastoral story of agricultural ownership. The story begins with a vast innocent continent, natural and almost magically alive, capable of inspiring us to reverence and awe, and yet savage, a wilderness. A good rural people come from the East, and they take the land from its native inhabitants, and tame it for agricultural purposes, bringing civilization: a notion of how to live embodied in law. The story is as old as invading armies, and at heart it is a racist, sexist, imperialist mythology of conquest: a rationale for violence—against other people and against nature.*
> —William Kittredge

IN OUR GRADE-SCHOOL textbooks and science classes, the elemental forces that shape the earth are both mystical and sensational. Hot, red, luminescent lava pours from volcanoes to make new floors of black rock. Wind scours this rock and water flows over it, until deep canyons are carved, until buttes are left standing like blasted statues.

Glaciers create valleys. The sediment of oceans becomes a plain. These forces are unimaginably slow. They are nonhuman. They are gods.

Only recently have we understood how much we equal these deities in our ability to change the earth. In the mid-twentieth century, the use of nuclear weapons brought us up to the level of Zeus casting lightning bolts. Now, at the close of the century, we know that our smallest human action—one tree cut down, one goat set out to graze, one child drinking from a Styrofoam cup—can be magnified millions of times to result in the deforestation of Asia, the desertification of Africa, the breakdown of ozone in the atmosphere. Like wind and water, we are elemental forces. We are five billion strong and growing every minute. With such power comes responsibility— we must now question our smallest human action.

Ranching in the American West is more than a historical heritage and an economic statistic. It is more than the sum of its parts: cows, corrals, semi-trucks. The myth of the cowboy has become part of us as a people and a nation.

Still it must be questioned. Is ranching a sustainable agriculture? Is ranching in climates with low rainfall and fragile environments a good thing to do? Specifically, should cows be grazing on our national forests, our national wildlife refuges, our wilderness areas, and other public lands in the West?

Denzel and Nancy Ferguson say no. Kill the cow, find the cowboy another job.

In 1983, it was the Fergusons who trumpeted the first call to get all cows off the public lands. The idea seemed radical at the time. Even other environmentalists thought it a little crazy, a little too strong. Still, in the next few years, a small but extremely interested audience began to read the Fergusons' book, *Sacred Cows at the Public Trough*. Slogans appeared. "No more moo by '92." "Cattle-free by '93." Those deadlines came and went, and grazing on the public lands was not significantly reduced. But the idea of removing cows from a national forest or a wildlife refuge—indeed, from all national forests and all wildlife refuges—no longer seemed so crazy. To some people it made perfect sense.

Denzel Ferguson was raised in the small town of Wallowa in eastern Oregon. The countryside here is stunning, the kind of snow-peaked, blue-laked, tall-pine scenery that can make a visitor pause and reassess. *Shouldn't I be living here?* one thinks. *Isn't this what my life is supposed to look like?* The Wallowa Valley originally was the home of Chief Joseph and the Nez Perce Indians. They fought hard to remain but were driven away, finally, painfully, in the 1870s. Sixty years after that, Denzel Ferguson went to school here, worked as a summer hand for neighboring ranches, and dreamed—for a year in high school—of becoming a dentist. Dutifully, the teenager even practiced crocheting so as "to make my fingers nimble." The first of his family to go to college, Denzel took a general zoology course, just for fun. Ten years later, he had a Ph.D. in zoology and was teaching full-time at Mississippi State University.

In Mississippi, Denzel Ferguson tested fish for their resistance to the pesticides used in nearby cotton fields. Some of these fish, he discovered, could live quite happily in highly toxic solutions. When these resistant fish were fed to someone higher on the food chain—say, a snapping turtle—the turtle died. Denzel began to testify at congressional hearings and to promote the regulation of dangerous pesticides.

It was the early 1960s. Martin Luther King was on TV. The civil rights movement burned in the heart of the South. At some risk, Denzel spoke out against segregation and racial prejudice. He and his wife joined a church so that they could adopt two children; they left when the congregation refused to admit black people. In the heat of those Mississippi summers, Denzel thought often about the snow-capped mountains of the Wallowa Valley. As the years passed, he regretted that his son had never been trout fishing. He decided to go home.

By 1972, Denzel was divorced and the manager of Oregon's Malheur Field Station on the Malheur National Wildlife Refuge. The station, which offers classes in the spring and summer, is funded by twenty-two colleges and universities. Its main draw is Malheur Lake, the largest freshwater marsh in the country and a major breeding ground for thousands of wild ducks, geese, egrets, cranes, herons, pelicans, swans, and other birds. Peregrine falcon and the northern bald eagle hunt these fields. Some twenty-five thousand humans visit the refuge every year.

Nancy was a twenty-year-old cook at the field station who would later become its assistant director. She had spent her childhood in rural Montana and Oregon "shearing sheep, milking cows, and bucking hay." She and Denzel soon married.

Up to this time, neither had ever given grazing a second thought. Like most westerners, they grew up with the lolling form of a Hereford or Angus in every pasture and creekbed. Cows were ubiquitous. They were part of the equation.

Certainly this held true at the Malheur National Wildlife Refuge, where virtually every available acre was grazed or mowed for hay. In 1972, livestock here reached a high of 125,000 AUMs. In government language, AUM stands for Animal Unit Month—the amount of forage required to feed a cow, a cow and her calf, or two yearlings for thirty days. If cows are grazing year-round, 125,000 AUMs is divided by 12 and amounts to some 10,400 mother cows. At Malheur, the cattle came onto the refuge in late fall and stayed until early spring—approximately six months of grazing or haying for 20,800 cows. Grazing was more than allowed; it was promoted as a management tool that stimulated plant growth and opened up feeding areas in meadows.

At that time, Denzel and Nancy Ferguson might have agreed with this idea. They had not yet connected the effects of long-term, heavy grazing at Malheur Lake to the drastic decline of early nesters such as mallards, Canadian geese, and sandhill cranes. As the cows ate off last year's growth, these birds could no longer find the cover they needed for their eggs. The exposed or poorly concealed nests were easily found by predators. In addition, cattle were trampling roosting sites. Fences divided feeding grounds. The haying of fields killed young birds caught by machinery. In 1948, with AUMs at about 75,000, waterfowl production was 151,000 ducks; in 1974, at nearly twice those AUMs, that number had fallen to 21,300.

More and more visitors began to complain about the lack of wildlife on the wildlife refuge.

"The cows were eating it up," Denzel Ferguson says now. "But you know, Nancy and I didn't see it ourselves. We humans can live in a deteriorating condition, and if the process is slow, we don't notice. As a man, I go and shave my face every day in the mirror. When I look at myself in that mirror, I still look the way I thought I looked at twenty-five. I don't see the changes because I have seen myself every day and I've learned to live with those changes. But if I saw myself in 1953 and then came back forty years later to shave again, why, my god! I'd have a heart attack!"

Unwittingly, this could serve as the apologia for western ranchers, who often have a hard time seeing a landscape they have known all their lives.

The Fergusons had no vested interest in ignoring their visitors' complaints. They looked a bit more closely at nesting sites. They counted 450 miles of barbed wire fence—festooned with the skeletons of snared deer, pronghorn antelope, and large birds. They listened to the assistant refuge manager "sit on our davenport and weep because cows were knee-deep in mud in his favorite birding site." They began to question the use of cattle as a management tool. They wrote articles. They talked to their friends. They campaigned to get some of the cows off the refuge.

The response from ranchers was violent. One Saturday night, the Fergusons were thrown out of a local dance and given the mythic western warning: "If you're not out of the county by Wednesday, you're dead." There were telephone calls every night. "A bunch of us guys are coming over to get you," said one blurry voice. "And who did you say is calling?" Nancy asked sweetly. Clearly an amateur, the man gave her his name. That was funny. But most of it wasn't funny at all. Small children began phoning too, little six- and seven-year-olds mimicking their parents' tough talk. The talk became tougher. "We're coming to get you now!" someone might say. Soon, a pickup would rumble slowly by. The Fergusons, who lived thirty miles from town, got out their hunting rifles.

Meanwhile, both the county and state cattleman's associations asked the Malheur Field Station to dismiss Denzel and Nancy from their jobs. When that failed, the ranchers worked in the state legislature to deny funds to the station.

The Fergusons were impressed. They wondered what "skeletons in the closet" these ranchers had. They got out more guns: soil erosion studies, grazing statistics, rangeland reports, wildlife numbers. In 1982, they quit working at the Malheur. They were afraid they had become a political liability to their employers. They also wanted to write a book.

Sacred Cows at the Public Trough is now in its sixth printing. Denzel admits cheerfully that *Sacred Cows* is biased. It makes no attempt to give the other side. That, he says, is what we have all been listening to for far too long.

Clearly, the Fergusons have become resistant, not only to the myth of the cowboy but to nearly every form of ranching nostalgia. This may follow logically from years of death threats. Still, their iconoclasm can be startling.

"Ranchers were the law of the land," Denzel says, "and they don't like giving up that power. Why, they used to kill a man for stealing a cow! What kind of civilized people would do that?

"In a rural community, ranchers are the big landowners. They're the big shots. They're arrogant and elitist.

"In these little western towns, you know, the smart ones leave. The dumb ones stay and become county commissioners.

"Ranchers cry out that we're ruining their livelihood. Why, a drug dealer could say the same thing. Oh, don't make me stop selling drugs! It's my way of life! That's probably what the plantation owners said. Oh, don't make me give up my slaves! It's my way of life!

"The relationship a rancher has with the land is superficial. He sees that hill and it's green and he sees forage for cows. I see shooting stars, balsam root, bunchgrass. I can name those plants and birds. Ranchers don't know those things. They don't have any appreciation for the lizards, the little mammals, the whole marvelous ecosystem. Who appreciates nature more? The person who looks at a flower or the man who sends out a steer to eat it?

[margin handwriting: Who's more virtuous]

"I've talked to ranchers. But they don't want to talk about what I'm talking about. They don't want to talk about soil erosion. They don't want to talk about changes in vegetation due to overgrazing. They don't want to talk about what happens when you clear-cut streams with cows. For one thing, they don't know enough about it. They've also got an inkling that they're guilty as sin.

"Ranchers stand and say how much they love the land. Well, if you're going to believe that just because they say it, I'll tell you that when the sun goes down I put on a Superman suit and fly around the valley. Are you going to believe that too?

"We got the cows at Malheur reduced to fifty thousand AUMs. But those numbers are climbing again. You can't turn your back. Leaving a few cows in a national forest or a wildlife refuge is like a surgeon leaving a few cancer cells. Those few can always become a lot.

"I have no sympathy for cowboys. Cowboys can go find something respectable to do. They can start by tearing down the fences from our public lands."

Denzel and Nancy live in a narrow corridor of private land in the Malheur National Forest in northeastern Oregon. For twenty miles, a dirt road follows like an obsequious hound the middle fork of the John Day River. The road and the glistening river pass close to the Fergusons' small green house with its satellite dish and white bunnies hopping in the yard. The bunnies are leftovers from a grow-your-own-meat scheme that didn't work out. The satellite dish is a rare extravagance. At the age of sixty-three, Denzel is retired. At forty, Nancy substitutes for the rural mail carrier and does odd jobs. In small ways, they live off the land, hunting deer and elk to put in the freezer and buying permits for picking mushrooms.

Like all national forests, the Malheur is grazed. If the Fergusons still talk about cows "every day of the year," it may be because they live daily with the presence of cows. Nancy says that the John Day River used to be a major salmon stream. But the impact of cattle eventually caused the disintegration and collapse of its banks. As the river became wider and shallower, the water temperature rose. In August, that temperature now goes to above eighty degrees, higher than salmon can withstand. Sometimes the river nearly goes dry.

The effect of cattle on riparian areas is well documented. Unlike wild ungulates such as deer and elk, cows tend to stay near water, to wallow in it, to lounge on the stream banks, and to trample the same ground over and over. As they lounge, they eat—grasses, tree shoots, whatever they find. On the John Day River, they eat, steadily, the willow and red-osier dogwood that act to slow the force of floods and protect the banks. They eat the grass that shields the soil from sun and wind, keeping soil temperatures low and reducing evaporation. They eat the sedges that are filtering out sediment, cleaning the water, and building up banks at the same time.

When this kind of vegetation is overgrazed, the look of a stream changes drastically. Trees such as willow, aspen, alder, and cottonwood disappear as mature trees die out and the young shoots are consumed. In areas with deep alluvial soil, the stream begins to downcut, creating deep channels that result in a lowered water table. Where streams have gravel or rock bottoms that resist downcutting, the channel becomes wider and shallower; like the middle fork of the John Day, it can no longer support many types of fish and wildlife. In both cases, a perennial stream can be transformed into an unstable, semipermanent trickle.

That cows often are the cause of this is not disputed. A 1988 report from the U.S. General Accounting Office (GAO) states baldly that many of our western riparian areas are "in degraded condition, largely as a result of poorly managed livestock grazing." (The GAO was established in 1921 to independently audit and evaluate government agencies. Some ranchers distrust its findings. But in a range war fought mainly with words, GAO reports remain the most neutral source of information.)

A few hours' drive from the Fergusons' house is a demonstration project called the Camp Creek Exclosure. These six miles of a badly eroded creek were fenced in against cattle, seeded for grass, and planted with willow between 1966 and 1974. The exclosure is a dramatic picture of what happens to a stream when cows are removed for over twenty years. At Camp Creek, alder, sedges, and rushes came back quickly to catch sediment; eventually the stream channel rose more than six feet. This, in turn, allowed the water table to come back up, which allows for trees and shrubs such as hawthorne and cottonwood. A higher water table means a continuous stream flow that can support fish such as rainbow trout and sculpins. The protected area also attracts an abundance of mammals and birds: raccoons, water shrews, mule deer, elk, voles, dippers, kingfishers, yellow warblers, and thrushes. Strikingly, outside the enclosed area, Camp Creek seasonally goes dry.

Denzel and Nancy feel strongly that overgrazing in the uplands also damages the watershed. When the cattle eat off the protective blanket of grass and compact the ground with their hooves, rain and melting snow course down the hills instead of sinking into the earth. Topsoil is carried away to muddy the John Day River, making it even harder for fish to survive. The left-behind gullies help lower the water table as underground water drains into the incised channel and evaporates.

"If you took the cows off, we could have the inland water supply of the pre–1900s," Nancy says firmly.

"We could have more salmon, more trout, more of everything," Denzel adds. "When they herd those cows by my house now, it takes five to ten minutes for them to pass. I like to imagine how many elk could pass by instead. Every spring Nancy and I see the elk and deer carcasses lying around. There's no forage for them. They've starved. In winter, we look outside the window with our binoculars and watch those elk paw through the snow, and I want to wave and say, forget it, guys. Forget it. It's all gone."

With the air of someone engaged in mischief, Denzel and Nancy say they can take any hunter and turn him into a "rabid cow hater" in ten minutes. I believe them. Denzel impresses with his vitality and conviction. Nancy has a phenomenal memory for facts.

I give her a test. What, statistically, can she tell me about public-lands ranchers?

Nancy says that many of them ranch for supplemental income. In 1990, 45 percent of BLM permittees and 35 percent of Forest Service permittees had less than one hundred cows.

Some ranchers, of course, are big time. Ten percent of BLM and 19 percent of Forest Service permittees use nearly half of the public land. These include "ranchers" like the Vail Ski Corporation, Union Oil, and Getty Oil. In the 1970s, ranches were a good tax shelter, and a number of wealthy people also bought them as a way to lose money. Absentee owners are still common today. Fourth-generation ranchers make good copy, but they are not the norm; less than 15 percent of permits issued by the BLM and FS remain with the family to whom they were originally given.

Nancy is concerned about sedimentation. She mentions a Colorado study that showed a 75 percent increase in soil erosion on grazed watersheds compared to ungrazed ones.

She talks about welfare ranching. In 1992, the grazing fee on the public land was about $2 per cow per month. (This number will certainly go up in 1993 under a new political administration.) Private-land leases typically are three or four times higher. In 1990, the federal agencies spent over $52 million more on programs dealing specifically with livestock than they collected in grazing fees. The government, in effect, must constantly pour funding into water tanks, pipelines, fencing, and management to repair and prevent the damage being done by cows.

"We're losing money," Nancy says. "Stupidly."

The Fergusons have had nearly twenty years to develop a fine sense of black humor when it comes to cows. "Give 'em a disposable diaper to eat," Denzel confides, "and their insides gum up. They die like *that!*" He laughs in appreciation. His anger is kept sharp, honed, and ready to use.

For all their show of cussedness, however, it is not rancor that fuels this couple. They are too healthy for that. Their chosen home—the curves of the John Day River, the stance of a blue heron, the sight of a bear in the evening light—all this is too beautiful for that.

Denzel tells a story about a conference he attended in Germany as a young professor. He had been working on the solar orientation of amphibians and was explaining an experiment that involved the handling and releasing of two thousand cricket frogs. Afterward, a German scientist came up to him in wonder. Denzel had seen two thousand frogs? He could go out in the field and catch two thousand frogs? He, the German scientist, had seen only four or five frogs, maybe six or seven, in the wild.

"They didn't even have frogs anymore!" Denzel exclaims. "How many species are we willing to give up in our country? How many can we give up and still have a livable planet? Once you go down that road . . . "

In a rare rhetorical moment, Denzel leaves the thought unfinished. He has spent much of his life outdoors—hunting, fishing, observing, pointing out animals and flowers to tens of thousands of students and visitors. He is full of a love that transforms immediately into strong words.

"I have seen things that my children will never see, and as for their children, hah! *Hah!* We have a responsibility that's beyond the personal. I can't sit by and watch people destroying what we have. We can still save the West. We're lucky. But every day we wait, we lose a few more options. Every day we wait, a few more solutions are no longer possible."

"It's our kids and grandkids who we should be thinking about," Nancy says. "Not twenty-three thousand permittees."

I listen and nod and mention that ranchers, too, often bring up their kids and grandkids. They say that, as a country, we can not afford to lose the cultural values of the small western town. If public-lands ranching is discontinued, ranchers believe that local economies will be devastated. Whole communities could be destroyed. What will the rural West look like then? Who will we be saving the West for?

Denzel leans forward in his chair.

As a teenager in a small, macho ranching and logging town, this man crocheted tea towels to prepare for a career in dentistry. This may seem eccentric. It may seem courageous. For Denzel Ferguson, it was simply pragmatic.

It makes sense, then, that his solution to the future of the rural West is also pragmatic and businesslike, without a shred of romantic pretense.

"Our whole exploitation of natural resources has to change," he says. "We can't keep exporting the land for money. In the new West, we have to look to tourism. We have to start saving ecosystems that can't be saved anywhere else. We could have huge chunks of wild scenery. We could have huge populations of wildlife. Let people come see it! We'll sell them gas, film, hot dogs, whatever. In terms of resources, tourists are nonconsumptive. They want a nice restaurant and a nice drink and something to look at. Tourists don't shoot up signs with their twenty-twos or overgraze or clearcut or drive up hillsides on their four-wheelers. Local people do that. Tourists don't take the resource away with them. Tourism. Retirement. Clean industries like the computer business with employees who want to go out and hike and fish and recreate. It won't be the same lifestyle for the rural West. It won't be the kind of growth that some people want. But you can't have growth from nothing. *We have to do what nature permits us to do.*"

"How much economic impact can twenty-three thousand permittees really have?" Nancy returns to that compelling number, worrying it mercilessly, tapping it like a cat to see if it won't move or explode or disappear. "I don't believe we'll miss them."

Denzel lights another cigarette. Both he and Nancy smoke like fiends. "I don't not eat beef for health reasons!" He smiles at me. "It's purely political. With all the smoking and the pesticide work I've done, I'm not going to lead a very long life."

He moves to the edge of his chair, a lean man, intense, serious.

"All of us would like to sit back and solve these problems so that everyone is happy and no one gets hurt. That would be nice. But we all know that human problems aren't solved that easily. It can't be done with pesticides or with grazing or with any other issue. Someone has to pay. Change is reality. Cows in the West are a stupid tradition. They don't make sense anymore. Cows on our public land are destroying our soil, our water, our wildlife—and we're giving them subsidies to do it! Let's kick them off! Every single one!"

"It's just a matter of time," Nancy says more softly. "It's just a matter of telling people the truth."

"The end is nothing; the road is all."
—*Willa Cather*

The Fergusons' truth, as they see it, has inspired a growing number of activists to carry on the torch of *Sacred Cows at the Public Trough.* Johanna Wald from the Natural Resources Defense Council,

Rose Strickland from the Sierra Club, Jim Fish from Public Lands Action Network, photographer George Wuerthner, Steve Johnson from Native Ecosystems, lawyer Joe Feller in Arizona—these are well-known names among the circle of environmentalists beginning to close in on public-lands grazing.

Most fervent of all, perhaps, is Lynn Jacobs. Once, on receiving a small inheritance, Lynn bought one thousand copies of the Fergusons' book and sent it free to anyone who would pay postage. In 1991, he self-published his six-hundred-page *Waste of the West: Public Lands Ranching,* the definitive word on antigrazing. Lynn typed his book out for three years on an unstable computer in an unair-conditioned trailer in Tucson, Arizona. As his health and finances declined, he yearned to give up his obsession for a back-to-the-land lifestyle in the rural Southwest.

"My heroes are the people who simplify their lives," Lynn Jacobs says. "The ones who get out of the system."

Despite their mutual interest, none of these environmentalists should be confused with any of the others. Lynn's ideal of a world in which humans return to a gathering society would baffle some of his colleagues. Denzel writes "nasty letters" to Rose Strickland, in which the Earth First!er urges Sierra Club Rose "to get on with the fight" or "get out of the way." Johanna Wald works in an office in San Francisco; Nancy Ferguson is as far from a city as most people get.

Still, in the spectrum of public debate, these men and women stand at one end. Their voices have a certain clarity and forcefulness. They know what they want.

Somewhere in the middle, somewhat less clear and less forceful, are Steve and Nena MacDonald of southwestern New Mexico.

The MacDonalds live with their two children in a rural community sixty miles from my own home in the Mimbres Valley. A short walk from their house is a stretch of the Gila River owned by the Nature Conservancy; this land adjoins the Gila National Forest. When the MacDonalds bought their two acres in 1986, their first impression was one of diversity. This area is a transition zone between the Rocky Mountains and Chihuahuan Desert. The uplands are a southern edge for elk and beaver, a northern one for coatimundi and peccary. In this rugged jumble of mountains, mesas, and canyons, the vegetation is a patchwork: spruce-fir, aspen, and ponderosa pine forests; oak and pinon-juniper woodlands; southern slopes of yucca and mesquite; deciduous willow, ash, sycamore, and cottonwoods along the stream banks. Rainfall is scanty, about fifteen inches a year. Eighty percent of the wildlife depend on the Gila River, which from its headwaters in the Black Range and Mogollon Mountains branches quickly into three main tributaries. These green veins carry the land's lifeblood.

Downriver from the MacDonalds' home is a country painting of irrigated fields, snaky lines of *acequias,* and black cattle. Here and there are pastures now dry because the water rights have been sold to the Phelps Dodge Mining Corporation. Past this section of private land, entering the southern portion of the Gila National Forest, the Middle Box of the Gila River includes the Bird Habitat Management Unit and Research Area, set aside in 1970 for its populations of black hawks, ducks, kingfishers, elf owls, and Gila woodpeckers. Beside these curves of water, coyotes yip and howl at sunset. Mountain lions leave their scat. Mule deer come to drink shyly.

Nena MacDonald is a nurse. Steve MacDonald is a wildlife biologist. They thought they could live here quite easily. But as they began to hike around, upriver and down, their focus began to shift—from diversity to damage. The damage clearly was being caused by cows. In 1989, Steve and Nena formed a small conservation group called Friends of the Gila River, made up of neighbors who owned land near or on the river itself. First, the group pushed the Forest Service into enforcing its management plan on the Bird Habitat and Research Area. For twenty years, trespassing cows from nearby ranches had overgrazed the "protected" riparian zone. Friends of the Gila River watched for these cows, made phone calls, wrote letters, and pointed out places where the fences were down. With a group of schoolchildren, they pole-planted willow along the denuded stream bank. Without the pressure of grazing, young sycamore and cottonwood soon sprang up like so many victory flags. A variety of birds started to nest in the area. Friends of the Gila began fencing out more illegal cows on the land owned by the Nature Conservancy. They pole-planted more willow. They became convinced of the virtue of physical labor. *Just get out and do it,* they thought. They felt exhilarated. They had fire in their eyes.

Pole-planting is a metaphor.

To restore riparian areas, branches of native *Salix exigua*—unimpressive knobby sticks about six feet long—are "planted" to the depth of the water table. These reintroduced trees represent the particular. As they leaf and root, they are meant to shade one particular river, to withstand the force of a particular flood, to fall prey, perhaps, to a particular beaver. Pole-planting means community as the willows encourage and are enhanced by a complex of grasses, insects, birds, and small mammals. Pole-planting is a gesture of healing. It is a laying on of human hands in an effort to restore what humanity has diminished.

In 1990, Friends of the Gila River collected three hundred names on a petition asking the Forest Service to make the restoration of the entire Gila River a priority. The conservation group cited the National Environmental Protection Act (NEPA), passed in 1969, which mandated that federal agencies listen to public input and encourage public action. Less than a year later, the district ranger's office sent out over four hundred letters requesting comments on the need for a new Upper Gila Riparian Management Plan. This plan would encompass three grazing allotments—the Watson, the Brock Canyon, and the Redstone—starting at the border of the Nature Conservancy's land and stretching north through the Gila National Forest into the Gila Wilderness.

More than one hundred people wrote back. Most targeted livestock as a major cause for the river's decline.

"The cheapest and most effective management tool is to stop grazing," declared one man.

"We do *not* want miles of new fences in the wilderness," warned another.

At the same time, the permittees and their relatives also wrote, saying that periodic flooding, low rainfall, and poor soil conditions were what really affected changes on the river. They believed that peccaries (piglike mammals native to the area) and motorized recreational vehicles caused more problems than cows. They quoted from rangeland studies showing that deer, rabbit, quail, dove, songbirds, and raptors actually preferred grazed to ungrazed areas.

Finally, one woman ended her letter plaintively, "New people who have moved into an area try to change everyone's way of living and they upset entire communities, even counties. Most are vegetarians and are against the ranchers. These people are leftovers of the 'hippie' age and want the land for themselves. . . . "

The Forest Service responded with an ID, or interdisciplinary, team, also known as an integrated resource management, or IRM, team. The group was a mix of private citizens and public officials. Its job was to list concerns that included problems in range management, watershed, recreation, and law enforcement. The team's report would assess a variety of management plans—from a reduction in cow numbers to the construction of new water tanks. These would be considered when the Forest Service supervisor made his final decision.

Purposefully eclectic, the IRM team consisted of the permittees from the Watson, Brock Canyon, and Redstone grazing allotments; four men from different divisions of the Forest Service; a biologist in the New Mexico Fish and Game Department; a hunter from the Gila Fish and Gun Club; a representative each from the Audubon Society, Wilderness Society, and Nature Conservancy; a university professor whose position was paid for by the New Mexico Cattleman's Association; and three people, including the only woman on the team, from Friends of the Gila River.

Like pole-planters, these people now had to deal with the particular.

The Watson grazing allotment starts at the edge of the Gila National Forest and covers over 6,600 acres, of which 1,770 are considered too rough for cattle. In 1991, 123 cows grazed the remaining area year-round. Within the borders of the allotment are 535 acres of private land, where the parents of the permittee lived until recently. This ranching family goes back four generations. They are people for whom canyons and mesas have been named. They were ranching here before the Gila Wilderness was designated in 1924 and before Forest Service boundaries were set in 1892, and they know these stands of ponderosa pine, these hills of juniper and scrub oak, very well. They do not, now, make a living from their ranch. Instead, the son works as a foreman for the nearby Western Cattle Company, a subsidiary of Phelps Dodge.

Where the Watson allotment stops, the Brock Canyon allotment begins and continues past the national forest into the Gila Wilderness. Of these 6,624 acres, about a third also are considered ungrazable. There are 288 acres of private land, the "base property" that is always tied to a grazing permit. The rancher here is a cousin to the rancher on the Watson allotment: as that family grew, the holdings they passed on were divided among the children. Officially, in 1991 the Brock Canyon allotment also could run 123 cows year-round. But most of the grazeable land here is on the Gila River itself, which is so degraded—both by livestock and by a decade of heavy flooding—that the permittee voluntarily reduced his herd to forty head. This man, too, makes his living working for the Phelps Dodge Corporation. He and his cousin manage their ranches on the weekends, in their spare time.

At a small ravine called Wild Cow Canyon, the Brock Canyon allotment turns into the Redstone, a vast tract of nearly 68,000 acres stretching down toward Silver City and up to the Black Range. Much of the Redstone is also in the Gila Wilderness. This rancher bought his grazing permit, attached to 814 acres of private land, in 1986 and went into partnership with two sons-in-law. Buying such a ranch is costly. At that time, it was not uncommon to pay to the previous owner $72 for every AUM allowed on the Forest Service permit: on the Redstone, that would have been $518,400 for a ranch allowed to run six hundred cows for twelve months. This would not have included the price of the private land, of the ranch house and outbuildings, and of stocking the range with real cows—all of which could boost the cost to well over $1 million.

The economics of ranching determine how many cows ranchers can afford to stock on their leased land and how many they can afford not to stock. Economics determine how resistant ranchers are to changing their management plans. Economics determine how well the land is cared for.

In 1991, the rancher at Redstone ran 400 cows. If 60 percent of his mother cows successfully calved (a good figure for such rough terrain), he would have had about 240 calves to sell in the fall. In 1991, a four-hundred-pound calf sold for about $400. Thus, quite roughly, $96,000 might have been the rancher's gross income—minus $9,456 in grazing fees (at $1.97 per cow per month), other operating costs, and any debts on the ranch (which for a new owner can be considerable). In this case, the net profit then might be divided with two other ranch partners.

Using the same figures on the Watson allotment, the rancher could have made about $29,600 in 1991 for 123 cows, minus $2,907 in grazing fees, and minus other operating costs. The rancher on Brock Canyon might have brought in about $9,600, with $945 in grazing fees, as well as other expenses.

If ranchers make decisions based on money, so does the government. How much we know about our public land and how much we manage it depends on federal funding. The last time the Forest Service had money to evaluate the Watson and Brock Canyon allotments was in 1958. At that time, most of the acreage was rated as fair, a category below good and above poor. (These descriptions mainly reflect "forage value" and are determined by the amount of bare soil, the vigor of plants, and the plant species composition.) The Red-stone allotment was evaluated in 1962, with 1,514 acres listed as very poor, 22,640 acres listed as poor, and 22,055 acres listed as fair.

Those were the facts. They came wrapped around a subjective opinion with which almost everyone on the IRM team agreed. The Gila River was in trouble. In too many places, immature growths of cottonwoods, willow, and sycamore did not exist. Stream banks were eroded and cut, and gravel bars strewn with beached debris. Sediment washed down regularly to muddy the water and clog irrigation canals in the valley below. There was a sense of ugliness—suggesting, perhaps, that aesthetics can resonate with an intuitive knowledge of land health. The Gila River, the Southwest's last major undammed river, was ugly.

So far, what Friends of the Gila River do is not dissimilar to the "adopt an allotment" plan urged by many environmentalists. This strategy involves getting to know a grazing allotment: walking its boundaries, counting animals, taking photographs, measuring erosion, keeping a notebook. It includes poring over files at the local Forest Service or BLM office and talking to the people who work there. It climaxes in getting on an IRM or ID team to influence management decisions. Implicitly, the idea is for antigrazing environmentalists to counter the prograzing sympathies of ranchers.

For Steve and Nena MacDonald, however, it's not that simple. For them, the name Friends of the Gila River has a double meaning. In the early 1970s, both were introduced to the Quaker faith and Society of Friends. In 1984, after reading about the Friends' work with Central American refugees, Nena took a summer job at a church in Tucson. Within months, she and other members of the Sanctuary Movement were indicted for openly helping Salvadoran families across the U.S. border. The resulting court appearances were a long way from Lubbock, Texas, where Steve had started to earn a master's degree in museum science. That drive, from Texas to Tucson, took Nena through southwestern New Mexico many times. More and more often, she stopped to stay with Quaker families in the Mimbres or Gila Valley. In 1986, she was acquitted of all charges.

Quaker philosophy and Quaker language dominate how the MacDonalds talk about public-lands ranching.

"It's like wearing several hats," Steve says. "I feel strongly that I am an advocate for the river and for the land, a voice for the voiceless. But I also feel, when I am on an IRM team, that I have to let the process work. There has to be a dialogue. There has to be consensus for any durable solution. This is not the time to be warring with our neighbor the rancher or with the Forest Service. We see ourselves as peacemakers, weaving webs of connection. We are all rural people here. What we share is important."

"We've had to let go of our preconceived ideas," Nena continues. "If you come to the table with your own plan, then it's hard to give up what you already want. Lots of ranchers here have expressed concern about the state of the river. We can't assume that we know what this man thinks or that this person's job is more important to him than his ethical feelings. We need to listen, to break down the barriers. Polarization only adds to the problem. When the fear level goes up, ranchers entrench. The war escalates."

"There's no us and them," Steve says. "The public land is not just their responsibility. I am the public. I am responsible."

The IRM team for the Upper Gila Riparian Management Plan began meeting in the winter of 1991. Unlike the MacDonalds, the Forest Service did not even hope for consensus among this group. They only asked for a range of reasonable management plans. The team quickly divided into three main camps. One believed that the river was so damaged that any solution, short of eliminating all livestock, was no longer possible. Across the room, a few people maintained that a solution wasn't even necessary; the river was being managed just fine. Then Friends of the Gila would pipe up, the self-described Don Quixotes: "It ain't right, and it ain't hopeless." Pole-planting. Fence-building. One step at a time.

All these people together, meeting after meeting, for as long as it takes. This is the process that Steve and Nena are committed to. It is admittedly imperfect. In the summer of 1991, a drought deepened. The IRM team argued. The river got worse.

Finally, Forest Service officials removed all cows from the Brock Canyon allotment and put them, temporarily, somewhere else. For a while, the cattle grazed on a state elk refuge. Then a rumor started that the Forest Service was going to use a vacant allotment along the headwaters of the Mimbres River—the river that runs past my house. People like my husband and me felt betrayed. Among those of us who live near public land, the word is always out. "Don't hike Black Canyon. It's being grazed this year." Or "The cows are off Meadow Creek." Or "No, no, don't go up the Animas. It's a mess!" For various reasons, the Mimbres headwaters had been left largely ungrazed for over six years and now, like Camp Creek Exclosure, the stream was lush with young trees and shrubs. Sacrificing one river for another did not seem like much of a solution.

At the same time, the permittee on the Watson allotment began managing his livestock differently. Suddenly, no one saw the cows on Watson Mountain near the Gila riparian area. Where were they? Steve is candid. "Probably nuking Mogollon Creek."

Redstone, too, kept its cattle away from the Middle Fork of the Gila River. What was happening out there on those sixty-eight thousand acres of wilderness and national forest? It was hard to say. Cows were being moved around like peas under a shell. Wherever they went, they kept on eating.

Denzel Ferguson surely would have snorted. Everyone wanted everyone to be happy! No one wanted anyone hurt! But was that possible?

In Quaker parlance, Steve and Nena "don't have clarity" on this issue. They are trying, always, to sidestep their own prejudices.

Sometimes they think, like the Fergusons, that domesticated livestock simply aren't "the right animal" for the arid Southwest. Cattle are an introduced and exotic species. They have no business munching on willow shoots and young cottonwood. Kill the cow, find the cowboy another job.

Sometimes they think that grazing *is* possible, if the public is willing to invest the money and time it takes to do it right.

Nena mentions a woman named Maria Varela and her group Ganados del Valle (Flocks of the Valley) in northern New Mexico. In one of the poorest rural communities in this country, Ganados del Valle employs between twenty-five and thirty people who raise long-haired *churro* sheep and weave clothing and rugs from the wool. The focus is on traditional Hispanic livelihoods and products. The problem is where to graze these sheep. In 1989, in a form of civil disobedience, Ganados sheepherders illegally took their flocks into a state wildlife refuge that was closed to livestock. The conflict pits environmentalists and wildlife managers against a pastoral people whose roots here go back to the seventeenth century.

Steve and Nena know that other Hispanics and Native Americans also lease small grazing allotments in the West. Sometimes they run as few as eight or ten or twelve head. Unmanaged, these cows can do considerable damage. Yet, combined with woodcutting and farming and an odd job here or there, cows and sheep are part of the patchwork of a rural lifestyle. They are part of a culture, and cultural values can be part of how the land is protected. It was Ganados del Valle that prevented a local ski-resort development and that led the fight for strict subdivision laws.

Should subsistent public-lands ranchers, with deep and abiding connections to an area, be given special consideration? Do they have more rights than developers or environmentalists or hunters? Do they have, on a wildlife refuge, more rights than elk? More rights than trout?

Steve and Nena "don't have clarity" on this question, either. Not having clarity is a painful position to maintain. It is something the MacDonalds must work at.

"It's easy to get into a desperate mode," Nena says. "But that's a trap. You start thinking that things are so desperate you have to do whatever it takes to reach your goal."

"You can justify a lot of means if you have noble ends," Steve agrees. "But our job is to focus on the means. Grazing in the West has been going on for a long time. It's a bad situation, but it's not the kind of crisis that justifies *any* means or *any* solution no matter how wrong it is."

For Friends of the Gila River, it is wrong to deny to any rancher his or her due process of law. "Cattle-free by '93" does not make sense. Ranchers have been operating under a legal system of grazing on the public land. They have justifiable assumptions. We ignore these at the peril of our own.

It is also wrong to call names. The phrase "welfare rancher," which refers to the traditionally low grazing fee on federal land and the cost of the grazing management program, is calculated to infuriate people who see themselves as uniquely tough, independent, and self-sufficient. The rancher says "urban elitist" and the environmentalist replies "ignorant land-raper." Although such exchanges can be deeply satisfying, they are usually counterproductive.

It is wrong, finally, to point the finger in any direction but one's own. "Who in this society can afford to be holier-than-thou when it comes to ranchers?" Nena asks. "Middle-class America is probably doing more damage than ranchers will ever do. I have to look at my own lifestyle before I can talk about anyone else's."

"Some people accuse us of being co-opted by ranchers because we want to work with them," Steve says. "Co-option. Cooperation. I see a difference."

The MacDonalds' commitment is to community. They are concerned with what binds people into relationships. That concern is self-taught, conscious, and not entirely natural.

Nena grew up in Los Angeles. Steve grew up trapping animals in rural Minnesota. For different reasons, neither connected to the communities of their childhoods. Eventually, both traveled to Alaska, where they met, married, and tried to escape community altogether. On two separate occasions, a year each time, they lived "in the bush," a magical place they remember with awe and wonder. Twenty years ago, the Alaskan bush was a busy, luminous, pristine ecosystem that was still intact, still whole. Wolves howled in the night, and mink left footprints in the snow. For Steve and Nena, the wilds of Alaska set the scale, and no place has measured up since.

Naturally, they left. It seems we must prove, over and over, that we can only visit paradise. Simply put, they missed their own species. Their consciences, too, were not entirely at ease. "I couldn't sit and enjoy the last wilderness on the planet," Nena says, "while the rest of the world went to hell."

Steve MacDonald has his regrets. The grizzly bear in the Gila Wilderness was extinct by the 1920s. The wolf is gone from the Southwest, as are native jaguars, black-footed ferrets, and many other plant and animal species. In Arizona and New Mexico, 90 percent of the original riparian ecosystems have been lost. Sometimes, this country—the lower forty-eight states, the Gila River, his own two acres—looks too depleted for his heart to bear. The glass is half empty and emptying still.

Such thoughts prompted Steve to abandon his first plan for making a living in rural New Mexico. While Nena worked as a nurse, Steve hoped to open a nature center on the Gila River, a place for students and teachers and tourists. "It would have been an illusion," he says now. "A postage stamp to feel good about while the rest of this land deteriorated. Why bring hundreds of visitors into a delicate riparian area? Why impact this with more people?"

For Denzel Ferguson, a word such as *tourism* is as natural and neutral as a little brown bird. But when Steve MacDonald speaks of tourists, he does so with a pained expression.

"It would be the same old rich crowd, wouldn't it?" he asks rhetorically. "It's not some poor Navajo kid who's going to go traveling around in an air-conditioned motorhome using up gas."

"It's our standard of living that's the problem," Nena says, "and tourism is just another part of that problem! We've got to get more in line with the world and with our resources. We aren't paying the costs yet of all our energy use, of all the soil going down the river, of all the waste! But we will. Our children will."

In this, the MacDonalds agree with Denzel and Nancy Ferguson. They, too, see a poorer West, one with less growth. They see a world in which we do what nature permits us to do. They do not see this as bad. Community can replace consumerism. Gardens can replace grocery bills. Windmills can replace power stations.

Earnestly, imperfectly, the MacDonalds try to live up to their ideals. They recycle with fervor and live in a house made of adobe and straw bales: five hundred square feet that cost $4,000 to build. They still buy meat and grocery products. But with their garden and chickens and rabbits, they hope to become more self-sufficient each year. Steve does the work needed to keep a country home working. He is also an unpaid and nearly full time conservationist, a member of three different IRM teams. Nena works in town at the hospital. In part to avoid paying taxes that would go into weaponry and national defense, they keep their income below poverty line. They are the heroes that Lynn Jacobs admires. They are trying to simplify.

"I can understand ranchers who sneer at professional environmentalists with their expensive backpacking gear and expensive cars coming into the Gila Forest and telling us what to do," Steve says. "The head of the Nature Conservancy! His salary is ridiculous! That's not what this is all about."

Steve is coming dangerously close now to pointing his finger. And

Nena's speeches about a poorer, more sustainable West are dangerously close to a specific goal. With good humor and grace, they back
off.

"I'm trying to let go of figuring it out," Steve says, giving a laugh
that starts pleasantly in his stomach. "I want to focus on dealing with
people and with the land in a daily way. That's the work for me. How
do I treat my neighbors and these animals and this land? How do
we all stay connected?"

Although the MacDonalds' philosophy and lifestyle could well be
described as a "leftover from the hippie age," it could also describe
the values of local ranchers themselves. In their vision, too, a connection with the land is more important than material wealth.
Ranchers who have inherited a ranch, like the permittees on the
Watson or Brock Canyon allotment, usually have the option of selling their private land, surrounded by national forest, for a lot of
money—but this is not something they want to do. This land is their
home and community in a way that is irreplaceable. It is to their
credit that these men and women know what they have and love it
so intensely. It is to their credit that the MacDonalds recognize this
love.

By the fall of 1992, eighteen months after their first meeting, the
IRM team for the Upper Gila Riparian Area had only a draft report.
The Forest Service began to move ahead on its own, transferring the
cows on the Brock Canyon allotment to another unused allotment—not on the Mimbres River. For a long stretch, the Gila River
is now rested from cows. Meanwhile, the uplands of the Brock Canyon allotment are being used by the Watson Mountain permittee,
which should alleviate some of the pressure on that land. A new
fence crosses the allotment, and a water tank has been put in to help
keep the cows from the stream area. On the Redstone allotment, the
permittees promise that they, too, will cowboy their cows away from
the river; unfortunately, there are signs that this is not happening.

Steve MacDonald is pleased with some of these changes. He is also deeply and unexpectedly frustrated. He wonders if the IRM process was not a bit of a sham, something to keep him and others like him happy. He wanted more from the federal government: more dialogue, more communication, more consensual decision making. Lately, the cows have been trespassing again on the Bird Habitat Management and Research Unit. Fences are down, and the ranchers don't care. Frankly, says Steve MacDonald, the Forest Service doesn't seem to care either.

It's like pushing against the wind.

"I don't know how to make the IRM process a living and breathing thing," Steve admits. "I'm beginning to wonder how much help the federal agencies can really be. Change needs to be community based, I think, brought about by people who are already in place."

Steve is working on a new project, an ecosystem approach to management developed by private citizens outside the Forest Service. The rancher on this allotment is eager to cooperate. He's involved because he wants to be, not because it's required by the government. There's some pole-planting to do, some data collection, some things to work out.

"What we share is important," Steve and Nena say.

It is not a particularly forceful statement. But it is a thread to unravel. Who knows? It could be the one that leads us home.

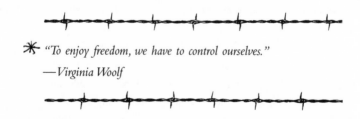

❋ *"To enjoy freedom, we have to control ourselves."*
—*Virginia Woolf*

Friends of the Gila River see the conflict between ranchers and environmentalists from a unique viewpoint.

There are many viewpoints.

Don Oman was raised on a farm near the Missouri headwaters and a state recreational site called the Madison Buffalo Jump. As a child, he looked forward every year to his family's single ritual vacation to Yellowstone National Park. At twelve years of age, he read a book about the Forest Service—he can't recall the title—that impressed him in the way books do when we are young and ready to shape our innate idealism. Like most male children on a farm, Don spent his summers lifting heavy, itchy bundles of hay. He is a man who cultivates humor and honesty. He guesses in an easy tone that he fell in love with being a Forest Service ranger because when he was eighteen and looking for a summer job, it was the Forest Service that got him out of the hot valley and into the cool mountains. There he sweated to maintain range fences and build water tanks for cattle. But afterward, he'd lie down with a sense of wonder "under the shade of a big tree to watch the squirrels."

Twenty-seven years later, Don Oman still likes all that—watching squirrels under the shade of a tree, hunting elk, fishing for trout, riding a horse in the high country. In his spare time, he paints oil pictures of these very things: elk, mountains, and trees. Although a career in the Forest Service usually requires a tour in Washington D.C., Don has managed to avoid that kind of promotion. He wants to "stay close to the ground" in management jobs like the one he has now, the district ranger in the Sawtooth National Forest near Twin Falls, Idaho.

When he was twelve years old, Don may have foreseen romantic adventure in Forest Service phrases such as "staying close to the ground" and "protecting the resource." Idly, childishly, he may have imagined people writing and calling him from across the country just to say thank you. Thank you, district ranger Don Oman, for doing your job! He may have fantasized about the newspaper articles, the TV shows, the movie offers.

More probably, this country boy did not think of these things at all.

Amazingly, they all happened.

For many westerners, the story of Don Oman has an odd piquancy. A district ranger? A Forest Service official? A bureaucrat? *A hero?*

The title "resource manager" is clearly pompous. Perhaps for that hubris alone, people like Don Oman have been caught in the middle, between environmentalists and ranchers, and reviled by both sides.

In terms of grazing, an environmentalist's history of the Forest Service and Bureau of Land Management might begin in 1891, when President Benjamin Harrison designated more than 13 million acres as forest reserves in seventeen western states and Alaska. President Cleveland set aside another 26 million acres in 1897 and Teddy Roosevelt another 132 million between 1903 and 1909. The need to do this was clear; the rampant abuse of range and timber in the West by private citizens horrified even Congress. For a while, the right to graze these new reserves was in doubt. In 1897, the General Land Office actually prohibited all sheep grazing outside of reserves in Oregon and Washington. The livestock industry was outraged, and the government's good intentions soon gave way before the wrath of powerful ranchers. During World War I, in the cry for more red meat, the public lands were even further overgrazed. As conditions declined, the Forest Service tried weakly to reduce stock numbers and enforce some system of regulation. Meanwhile, the Division of Grazing—now the Bureau of Land Management—sank deeper into the pockets of wealthy miners and cattlemen. Every attempt to protect the land, from the establishment of grazing fees to the issue of permits, was hard fought and hard won. Finally, in the 1960s and 1970s, major environmental legislation was passed: the National Environmental Protection Act, the Endangered Species Act, the Forest and Rangeland Renewable Resources Planning Act, and the National Forest Management Act, among others. These laws are laudable. The problem is enforcing them.

This is a history in which government wimps consistently cow-tow to the demands of commodity interests. It is a history of compromise and resource degradation.

A rancher's version of the same story would start a bit earlier, say, in 1872. A pioneer family comes out west to fulfill the American dream. The family homesteads by a small creek. They own this source of water, which they combine with the "open range" to make a modest living. Suddenly, the government starts seizing the common land. Eastern interests are at work. The West is losing control of its destiny. In 1906, the Forest Service begins to charge for something that has always been free. Grazing permits are issued. The Forest Service calls them "a privilege"; livestock owners call them "a right." Concerned about the future and health of their range, ranchers help pass the Taylor Grazing Act in 1934, which extends the grazing rules, organizes advisory boards made up of stockmen, and sets up the Bureau of Grazing and Mining. The fight against government interference continues. The Forest Service, especially, is composed of "college boys" and "paper pushers" who don't know which end of the cow to follow. The movement to lock out Americans from their own land grows stronger. In the 1990s, some ranchers launch the logical counterattack; they claim that the public lands are really a "split estate" in which they own certain property rights.

This is a history of harassment and unnecessary regulation. It is a history in which private citizens pit themselves against a powerful government and a mean-spirited ignorance.

Undoubtedly the truth lies in pieces, a bit here, a bit there, a large chunk somewhere else.

More clearly, the Forest Service and BLM are juggling knives. Their mandate is to manage more than three hundred million acres of public land for a variety of purposes, including outdoor recreation, range, timber, watershed, and wildlife. Many of these interests directly conflict. All this use—heavy use, at times—must be balanced with land health and a sustained yield of resources. *You can't get some-*

thing from nothing. Further, we expect this kind of graceful performance from one of the clumsiest organizations on earth—the bureaucracy.

Today, the Forest Service has a permanent work force of over thirty-five thousand people in professional, administrative, technical, clerical, and other positions. The system is divided into ten Forest Service regions, about eight experimental stations, and a number of offices in Washington, D.C. The BLM is a somewhat smaller operation. Many people consider these agencies to be understaffed.

As in other bureaucracies, the goals of the Forest Service and the BLM must be translated into a career, which requires a career ladder. Managers are expected to move from "on the ground" to supervisory desk jobs: they move laterally as well, from district to district, every few years. In this way, they gain a breadth of experience, make minor but measurable progress up the ladder, and are less likely to become co-opted by the local community.

The arrangement has its disadvantages. Ranchers complain that Forest Service and BLM officials are also less likely to get to know a local community or to understand the ecosystem of an area. They are unfamiliar with patterns of drought and flood. They start projects and never see them finished. They are insensitive to the native culture. They say the wrong thing to the wrong person at the wrong time.

In 1986, Don Oman fit the typical image of a Forest Service employee. He had served on eight different national forests, with experience in timber, range, silviculture, minerals, fire, wildlife, and recreation. He had received high recommendations and a number of awards, and he was known to work well with people. His new job on the Sawtooth put him in charge of 320,000 acres and thirty-four permittees on eighteen different grazing allotments.

At that time, most of the permittees on the Sawtooth National Forest had grazed cows there for many years, in some cases for many generations. They did things their way. Historically, the ranchers on

Goose Creek, for example, simply opened the fence gates and allowed livestock to drift through nearby BLM land into the national
forest, until all the cows had access to the 56,000-acre allotment.
These ranchers weren't used to moving their cattle in order to rest
certain pastures, nor to keeping cows out of certain creekbeds. They
didn't want to consider the interests of a distant public. Standards on
the Sawtooth, to understate the case, were low.

In the last ten years, however, the Forest Service had begun—from
the permittees' point of view—to change the rules. The emphasis on
protecting stream-lying areas was particularly new. The constant
herding of cattle involved more labor and manpower, as did the tanks
and pipelines needed to water cows away from the riparian zone. It
was hard to keep up all those fences and to move a herd according
to schedule. Inevitably, Don Oman's insistence on these things was
resented.

The permittees took it personally.

But Don Oman was simply reading Forest Service directives and
trying to follow them. In the 1980s, the U.S. General Accounting
Office and various congressional hearings highlighted range problems in the West. Eager to demonstrate its concern, the Forest Service adopted the slogan "Change on the Range" and encouraged its
employees "to protect the resource" more vigilantly than ever
before.

In the Sawtooth National Forest, Don began to take photographs.
These pictures showed it all: deepening gullies, soil erosion, dried-up
creeks—the basic western landscape.

Outside the Sawtooth, when Don Oman went to regional and
national workshops sponsored by the Forest Service, he was given
pages and pages of no-nonsense imperatives:

"Stop all basic resource damage caused by livestock!"

"Hold permittees accountable for livestock movement from pasture to pasture, for removal of livestock from NFS lands at the end
of the grazing season, and for maintenance of improvements. Don't

allow livestock onto forest if maintenance is not completed prior to turn-on date! Send them home if next pasture isn't maintained!"

"Be fair but firm! Don't bluff if violations occur, as this just convinces the permittee that we will not take action. Take suspension or cancellation action as is warranted. Don't make outlaws out of permittees by making hollow threats with no follow-up!"

Finally, one trainer on riparian management went beyond the ubiquitous exclamation point:

"I challenge each of you to exercise positive personal leadership. Above all, your attitude should reflect that riparian area stewardship is fundamental to our mission as an agency. IT'S THE RIGHT THING TO DO! FOR PEOPLE AND FOR RESOURCES!"

Don Oman believes in the rhetoric. He believes that when permittees sign their grazing permit each year, they sign on for a clear and specific management plan. The plan includes so many water tanks, so much pipeline, so much fence, and so many cows moved at such and such dates. Don explains that usually the government pays for materials used in developments like water tanks or new fences; the rancher pays for installation and maintenance. He notes, with emphasis, that the costs of such labor and of raising cows in harsh terrain are figured into the price of the federal grazing fee. That fee is tied, then, to the rancher's financial and emotional commitment to the management plan.

In Don's first year in the Sawtooth National Forest, he filed forty-five violations of a management plan on one allotment alone. One violation, in which cows were secretly moved to a sensitive creek area, could have resulted in cancellation of the permit. But Don's superiors took no action. Indeed, no action had *ever* been taken against a rancher on the Sawtooth for as long as anyone could remember.

Don persevered. He filed more violations and took more photographs. His file cabinets bulged. There are those who think that he went about his job badly, that he said the wrong thing to the wrong person at the wrong time. One rancher vividly recalls the district ranger's first tour of his allotment, in which Don declared, abrasively, that it was the worst one he had ever been on.

Still, other people describe Don Oman as the proverbial "nice guy," a concerned father of three sons, a faithful husband, a Sunday-school teacher, a man who could be wryly funny.

Local environmentalists, at least, began to like him a lot.

In the summer of 1988, the Forest Service announced yet another new and important policy change. District rangers in the Sawtooth National Forest were given the power to suspend or cancel part of a permit for violations of its terms. Don Oman no longer depended on his superiors for action. After the required number of warnings, the ranger suspended 10 percent of one grazing permit for two years, subject to appeal. The ranchers had not maintained a fence that was protecting a burned area, had not moved their cows from one unit to another by the agreed-on date, had not repaired the fence between Forest Service and BLM boundaries, and had not had certain pipelines and water troughs ready. Don warned other permittees: the same thing could happen to them.

The number of meetings—between rancher and rancher, rancher and ranger, the ranger and his staff, the ranger and his supervisors— increased dramatically.

One confrontation with the Wild Rose permittees was fairly typical. Don Oman said that the permittees were too possessive of the public land; for example, they had not asked for clearance before constructing an addition onto a holding pasture. The rancher replied that this was simply the American way of doing things. It was un-American to ask!

In another instance, a range conservationist chastised a permittee about putting in an unauthorized pipeline through six prehistoric Indian sites. "There will be repercussions," said the exasperated government worker, "but I guess you expected that when you decided to put in the pipe." The rancher's reply echoed his larger confusion.

"I guess I don't know what I expected, but I've put in a lot of pipe and never had to put up with all this archaeological crap!"

By this time, the ranchers had long pursued Oman's transfer. In a time-honored tradition, they requested it from their congressional representatives, two U.S. senators, the head of the Sawtooth National Forest, and the head of grazing for the Intermountain region. So far, they had been unsuccessful.

Then, in the fall of 1989, the range staff at the Twin Falls district heard from "a reliable source" that one of the Goose Creek permittees had too many cows on his allotment. Don arranged a surprise count. He assembled a team of two state brand inspectors, a BLM official, the Twin Falls range conservationist, and himself to meet at the Piney Cabin Corrals, where five permittees were rounding up their livestock. Another range conservationist flew a small plane to inspect the area for strays. Don already had received threats of physical violence. So two Forest Service law enforcement officers came along as well. A small Ryder moving van was taken as a camper.

At first, one of the ranchers cursed in Don's face, demanding to know what the district ranger was doing there. But the other permittees were more civil, and the count went smoothly. It would indeed show that one rancher was shipping more calves than he had permitted cows. No action against the man was taken. The Forest Service had made its point.

The more the ranchers thought about it, however, the madder they got.

In the *Western Livestock Journal* the story became "The Gestapo Cattle Count." The Ryder van had looked suspiciously like a paddy wagon. The armed officers and swooping plane had cast a pall over the day. One permittee later explained to a reporter from the environmental newspaper *High Country News,* "Gathering the cattle like that is our payday. It's also one of the few times we get to cowboy. And it's a family deal. Our wives come out and make a dinner. The children are there. . . . If a patrol car is parked in front of your house all night, your wife and kids would wonder: What did you do wrong, Dad?"

The Idaho Cattle Association requested the secretary of agriculture to investigate the count.

A sportsmen club asked the secretary to investigate grazing practices on the Goose Creek allotment.

Don's supervisors now were convinced that he could no longer work with local ranchers. At an informal meeting with the president of the Idaho Cattle Association, the president of the Idaho Public Lands Council, and three of the permittees, the Forest Service's regional director of range management promised that Don Oman would be transferred from Twin Falls within a year.

The district ranger did not hear of the deal directly. He learned of it roundabout, many weeks later. He understood, of course, that such agreements were common. These things happened every day, all the time, in every national forest. Resource managers were occasionally and simply transferred when they pushed local interests too hard. That wasn't new. But Don Oman's response was.

He consulted with his wife.

Then he filed a "whistle-blower's complaint" stating that Forest Service management and the livestock industry were preventing him from doing his job. His report was quite detailed. It included pages and pages of enthusiastic worksheets, urging him to "stop all basic resource damage done by cows" because "IT'S THE RIGHT THING TO DO! FOR PEOPLE AND FOR RESOURCES!"

The media became interested.

In the spring of 1990, the *High Country News* ran a lengthy piece on the problems of ranger Don Oman. The *New York Times* picked up the story and included a quote from one of the permittees. "Either Oman is gone," said one old-time rancher, a leader in the community and a millionaire, "or he's going to have an accident. Myself and every one of the permit holders would cut his throat if we could get him alone."

When asked if this was a threat on Oman's life, the man clarified, "Yes, it's intentional. If they don't move him out of the district, we will."

People magazine followed with a five-page article titled "The Lone Ranger Rides Again." The cut line was dramatic: "Despite threats from ranchers and betrayals by his boss, ranger Don Oman fights to save the Sawtooth National Forest." In that piece, the permittee amended his statement. "I didn't threaten to cut his throat," the rancher complained. "I said if he didn't quit, he'd have a wreck."

Audubon and *Wilderness* published their articles in 1991. Meanwhile, President George Bush interpreted the rancher's comment in the *New York Times* to be a public threat of a government employee. The war with Iraq had started, but a presidential aide found the time to begin a Justice Department investigation. Later, charges against the eighty-two-year-old permittee were dropped when the newspaper reporter refused to testify. The *Western Livestock Journal* rejoiced, but no one else really cared. What people cared about, the story behind the story, was the nuts and bolts of public-lands grazing.

By now, the investigator of Don's complaint had begun his interviews.

At least one former range staff officer from the Twin Falls district confirmed that many of the permittees there had a history of permit violations and were "very, very challenging to work with." The investigator noted that this officer still had a home and family in Twin Falls and "was careful and hesitant in his answer" as though "reluctant to speak freely."

When it was his turn to meet with the permittees, the investigator observed that these ranchers sincerely "believe that Mr. Oman is uninformed of range management and is systematically trying to undermine their 'rights' to graze cattle under their permit. Many believe that Mr. Oman is implementing new and useless management techniques to make their cattle operations unprofitable and to drive them off the public lands. Since this has a serious economic impact on each of the permittees, some react very emotionally and have difficulty discussing it rationally or objectively. The documented instances of threats in Mr. Oman's complaint are real and have occurred."

From Forest Service management, the investigator learned that Don Oman was, in fact, a good employee. It also was true that guidelines for the Sawtooth National Forest were not being met. And yes, Forest Service supervisors had told ranchers they would transfer Don Oman. They felt that this was their prerogative. The permittees had made it clear—they would not cooperate with the district ranger.

Don Oman claimed that his efforts to enforce grazing regulations had not been supported by his superiors. On this point, the government investigator turned subtle. He described this only as a "very real . . . perception" on the part of many other Forest Service employees—as well as on the part of the permittees themselves.

The investigation concluded, however, that there was no "conspiracy" by Forest Service management to allow ranchers to violate the terms of their grazing permits. Nor is there anything that prohibits ranchers from pressuring politicians and agencies to fire or transfer a government employee. This, at least, *is* the American way. Finally, since the decision to transfer Don Oman had come before his whistle-blower's complaint, it was not an illegal reprisal.

By this time, the Forest Service had dropped the idea of moving their Twin Falls ranger. Until they pursued it again, Don had no further grounds for action.

There are two things that Don Oman communicates strongly about his last few years as a district ranger.

One is the pleasure he gets from helping restore rangeland and riparian areas. Soon after Don came to Twin Falls, he went to Oregon to see the Camp Creek Exclosure by Denzel Ferguson's house. It was an exciting trip. Indeed, a main complaint from Sawtooth ranchers is that after seeing Camp Creek, Don returned to Twin Falls and tried to duplicate its success. He tried to demonstrate, through his own projects, that removing livestock from a stream could result in obvious improvement.

"These areas have an amazing ability to recover," Don says with parental pride. He points to the photo of a creek that he and local conservationists fenced off from cows. "Look at the sedge grass there! Look at the sediment being caught!" As Don talks, his hands hold the weight of that valuable soil. They curve to show how the water table leaches into a deepening gully. They fly up at the wonder of stream restoration.

Don's scrapbook of pictures is like a family album. In an ungrazed section of Trapper Creek, the banks have dense stands of willow with massive root systems that protect the stream from floods; three hundred feet away, outside the exclosure, the ground is eaten bare by cows. Look! Don exclaims, here is Shoshone Creek! Here is Squaw Creek! Here is Trout Creek! Gosh, Trout Creek . . . how many old western streams are named for the trout they can no longer support? Here is a little experimental cage enclosing a patch of ground. Look inside, Don says, to see how quickly willows grow when they are not being grazed.

Don Oman has tried to show ranchers why riparian areas need to be improved and how that will ultimately benefit them. The response to this education—the slide shows, the photographs, the lectures—is mixed.

"He treated us like naughty sixth graders," one man complained to the *High Country News.*

"These ranchers are farmers, too," Don says. "They have private land where they grow supplemental crops for their cattle and for sale. Some of them just want that water to rush down the creeks and gullies into the reservoir. They think they'll have less irrigation if we hold more water up here in the hills. But it's just the opposite! We could have ten times the amount of late-season water available if we stopped erosion and got the water table back up. Some of these ranchers have good ideas. And they know every inch of their ranch. But they see things only from their perspective. When it comes to putting cows on the spring or fall range, they don't see the needs of the land. They just want the cows out of their fields—so they can start growing crops or haying."

Don is quick to explain that he is not antigrazing.

"I think we can have cows on the public land if they're managed right."

As a manager, Don Oman is in an enviable position. His whistle-blower's complaint and the press coverage that followed ensure that he will not be wrongfully removed from his job. The Forest Service has even given him permission to speak officially, as a Forest Service employee, about grazing issues.

This is the second thing that Don Oman radiates: a sense of freedom. Unlike most people in the Forest Service or BLM, he is happy to talk to writers and reporters. A stuffy room is being aired. Dark blinds have been pulled up. Windows have been flung open! Don Oman feels that he has nothing to hide. He loves his profession. He feels that it, too, should have nothing to hide.

"Unscrew the locks from the doors," Walt Whitman wrote. "Unscrew the doors from the door jambs!"

"I'm at the height of my career," Don says happily. "My lifetime goal was to become a district ranger and to have an effect on the resources. I get hundreds of phone calls and computer messages, from environmentalists and government people who also want to see these changes. They are glad I spoke out. If I retired tomorrow, I'd be pleased."

In 1992, Don Oman was still the district ranger in Twin Falls, Idaho. He believes that his working relationship with many local ranchers has improved. Most of the fences and water developments are finally working, units are being cleared of cattle when not in use, and the distribution of cattle is better. The district has a new forest supervisor and a new regional forester who have pledged to support any efforts to "protect and improve the resource."

"Right now, my wife and I have no plans or desires to leave," Don says.

If he did leave and if he stayed in range management, I wonder if he would find the same problems elsewhere. Are ranchers across the West ignoring the rules of their grazing permits? Are they intimidating government officials? Are they blind to the needs of the land?

Or were the ranchers on the Sawtooth an exception?

"I don't think they are an exception," Don speaks quietly.

This is not quite the same as saying they are the norm.

Insiders in the Forest Service refer to "the Don Oman thing" as a milestone. It is beginning to happen on other forests, in Montana and Nevada, in Utah and California. In 1993, new political appointees in Washington, D.C., make Don Oman and others like him expect even greater changes in the future.

"I do know that fear used to be our main motivation," Don Oman says. "The fear of political pressure, the fear of offending the livestock industry, the fear of risking our jobs. Our fear needs to be turned around. We need to reach a point where we're afraid not to protect the land. We need to be more afraid of *not* doing our job than we are of doing it."

"In this case," he gestures with pride, "perseverance paid off."

"There are people in our society who seem to believe that heroes and heroism are things of the past, or that heroism never really existed in the first place. In recent years they have turned their guns on the cowboy and have tried to do a job on him. But the heroism of the working cowboy isn't a joke. It isn't a put-on. It isn't something that has been cooked up by an advertising agency, and it isn't something that cheap minds will ever understand. Cowboys are heroic because they exercise human courage on a daily basis. They live with danger. They take chances. They sweat, they bleed, they burn in the summer and freeze in the winter. They find out how much a mere human can do, and then they do a little more. They reach beyond themselves."
—*John R. Erickson*

"Myth does not mean something untrue, but a concentration of truth."
—*Doris Lessing*

In 1976, Denzel and Nancy Ferguson were kicking cowpies at the Malheur Wildlife Refuge and listening to the wildlife manager "weep on their davenport" about the excess of cattle in nesting areas. That same year, Doc and Connie Hatfield bought a ranch in central Oregon, 150 miles from the refuge. The Hatfields had looked for a long time before buying these eight thousand deeded acres of high desert, with an attached permit to graze six thousand acres of BLM land. They were looking for an ecosystem that included the ruminant animal, a place where cows and ranchers could fit into the natural world.

Doc and Connie had ranched part-time in Montana, on irrigated land in the fast-developing Bitterroot Valley. There, Doc was a veterinarian who dealt too often with problems that could have been prevented—cows with weak eyes, cows not birthing properly, cows with bad udders. A good rancher would have culled those cows. A good rancher knew genetics and worked with the flow of nature, not against it.

Both Doc and Connie wanted very much to be good ranchers.

In Oregon, like every rancher in the West, they inherited the past. The uplands and riparian areas had been grazed, without rest, for more than a hundred years. Until 1974, ranchers who leased from the BLM had to provide on their own land a "hay base" for five months of the year. To meet this requirement, thousands of acres of high desert country, ill suited for farming, were plowed under and planted with rye. Today, when winter snow runs off these old fields, it sounds like a live stream rushing down the hillsides—a flood of water, quickly gone, carving out the gullies deeper each year.

"That water should be sinking into the ground," Connie Hatfield says. "We have those gullies now, and we have erosion. As they farmed this land, those old ranchers leached the soil for sixty years. They didn't know that. There's no point in blaming them. They were like everyone else, like we are. They worked with the system. They did what they thought was right at the time."

In 1982, after twelve years of ranching, the Hatfields felt pretty good about themselves. They moved their cows often. They watched their breeding lines. They worked well with the local BLM. When they heard that the controversial wildlife biologist Allan Savory was coming to speak at an Oregon livestock association, they invited the man over.

"We thought we'd show him what a great place we had," Doc says. "We thought we were way ahead of the game."

Allan Savory is an intense man from Zimbabwe (formerly Rhodesia) who promotes "a planning process" that he calls holistic resource management, or HRM. Savory refuses to use the word *system*. "All systems fail," he says. "A planning process and a management system are opposites."

HRM begins when people collaborate to form a goal. Allan Savory says, quite calmly—as though he were not contradicting the majority of modern range science—that "if the environment is one of seasonal and especially low rainfall, and if the people's goal requires high biodiversity, clear running streams, and abundant wildlife as well as rural prosperity, then often cattle, properly handled, are the only tool which can produce such a goal."

Savory believes that domesticated cows can imitate the positive impact of wild game on native grasslands. The trampling of wild ungulates, bunched by pack-hunting predators, historically served to break up soil and allow new grass seeds to establish. Savory asks: why not cow hooves? In addition, cows can break up old plants that in brittle environments—those with seasonal rainfall and periods of drought—do not easily decompose into nutrients. Instead, the old growth of the plant "chokes" it and inhibits photosynthesis. Without a healthy litter of decomposed material, the soil erodes and even fewer plants survive. Thus, Savory explains that no grazing can be as damaging to a grass plant as overgrazing.

"In such brittle environments," Savory says, "most of the aboveground vegetation dies every year and the carbon cannot cycle without a partnership between large animals, their predators, and insects and microorganisms. If large animals are removed or remain without pack hunters, then the carbon cycle malfunctions and most biodiversity is lost."

When Allan Savory came to the United States in the late 1970s, he told ranchers that they could double their stocking rate: more cows meant more hoof action and more grass for more cows. The management of these cattle, however, had to change completely. Af-

ter the animals severely grazed a pasture, they had to be moved before they could return to plants whose root systems would be damaged by a "second bite." First stimulated by intense pruning, the
grass then needed time to grow and recover. This meant that cows
had to be carefully herded or controlled with fencing. They also had
to be bunched to produce the right trampling effect. The growth
rate of the grasses had to be monitored daily—on one's knees, not
from a horse. Moreover, the entire ecosystem of the ranch had to be
considered: humans, wildlife, plants, soil, insects.

"The world is not linear," Savory says. "It is not mechanical. It
only works in wholes."

Born on a continent known for the devastation of its range, Savory is more appalled by the condition of North America. He is obsessed with the growing desertification of the earth. Against all
conventional thought, he insists that intense grazing combined with
"the action of the thundering herd" is the only answer. He is not
fond of cows. But he recognizes that they are more easily attainable,
manipulated, and transported than wild game.

"Wildlife can't do the job," he murmurs regretfully.

Allan Savory learned his lessons from the savannas of Africa. Here
one can imagine, where trees meet grassland, the evolution of our
species. One can see how pack-hunting humans moved across the
plain as a predacious animal. Later, certain tribes developed an intri-
cate symbiosis with domesticated livestock. In the twentieth century,
Africa is known as a land where men and women starve with horrific regularity. Perhaps this is why Allan Savory emphasizes that *people* must be part of the solution.

"We have to manage whole situations," he says. "That means we
have to get people involved. We have to sustain them by generating
wealth. We have to reintegrate people into nature."

At the Hatfields' ranch, the first thing Allan Savory did was go to
those old rye fields. He wanted to know if he could take a photograph. What a marvelous example of degraded land! What a catastro-

phe! It would be great for his slide show on the destruction of the West!

For Doc and Connie Hatfield, this moment was one of those crossroads, too fast for thought, not always noticed, and irrevocably passed. They had a choice. They chose to be more intrigued by Allan Savory than insulted. Perhaps this arrogant man from across the world, with his tweed cap and English accent, had something to teach them.

The truth was that Doc and Connie were a little bored with being ahead of the game. They were even a little bored with ranching. In 1984, they went for seven days to Allan Savory's Center for Holistic Resource Management in Albuquerque, New Mexico. They would go again, many times. They would revolutionize, subtly, their style of management. They would never, ever, Connie says, be in danger of being bored again.

To many people, Allan Savory's ideas are immensely appealing. He has placed ranching in the context of ecology; more, he has given it an ecological justification. Cows can be good for the land. Cows are a way for the land to recover, a way to roll back the desert and stop global warming.

"The public may win," Savory warns, "and ranchers will stop grazing on the public lands. But as those lands get worse, we'll end up bringing state-owned cattle back! You can't reverse the damage through rest. Conventional livestock grazing has always overrested part of the range even as it overused other parts. Rest is half the problem, not the solution."

Ranchers find this talk invigorating.

Environmentalists use another word.

Almost everyone agrees that better management of cows is better for the land. Still, Savory believes that what he calls brittle environments *need* cows or their equivalent to promote biodiversity and that almost all perennial grasses suffer from being ungrazed. Some biologists complain that Savory has oversimplified the ecosystems in North America. The old growth surrounding a bunchgrass can reduce photosynthesis. But in the Sonoran Desert, old growth may be important in reducing transpiration—water, not sunlight, is the limiting factor. In cold deserts, old growth may protect the plant from freezing weather. Most clearly, riparian areas serve us best as silt collectors and sponges that soak up and hold water, with shrubs, trees, and old growth an important part of that function.

It is logical that grass evolved with grazers. We now understand that predators and prey form a healthy circle. In some areas, however, fire might have been more important in the creation and maintenance of grassland, both natural fires and those set by Native Americans. Certainly, severe grazers such as bison and elk are not historically natural in all parts of the West. Early accounts of New Mexico and Arizona show lush systems of grass existing, apparently, with only moderate numbers of free-ranging deer, elk, antelope, rodents, and a variety of birds and invertebrates. What happened here?

What did not happen may be even more important. These plant communities did not coevolve with a monoculture of large hoofed mammals bred to stay within fences and linger stupidly near water holes. Perhaps the real question is whether domesticated cows *can* reproduce the effects of wild animals.

Unfortunately, most textbooks dispute Savory's ideas about the beneficial hoof action of cattle. In Africa, where "The Savory Method" and "Short Duration Grazing" have been used since the 1960s, reports are mixed. One article in a range journal concluded that "many ranchers" and "most range specialists" in Africa are disillusioned.

In America, the majority of scientists also refute heavy stocking rates. On the other hand, some research does show that long-term resting of a degraded range may not promote recovery either. For these areas, light or moderate grazing is recommended. Other controlled studies seem to favor livestock exclusion, especially if the goal is native biodiversity.

Savory responds that although researchers try to imitate holistic resource management, they end up reverting to grazing systems and rotations that inevitably fail. He points to two success stories, an eight-year-long trial in Zimbabwe and a commercially successful ranch in Namibia. Scientists, he notes, are buffaloed by the HRM planning process because it involves so many variables. HRM does not fit neatly into a research proposal.

"The most scary thing in the world is new knowledge," Allan Savory says. "If it's incremental, we applaud. But if it's really new, we skin the person alive."

In the American West, the term *HRM* is becoming more popular every year among ranchers. The problem may not be what Allan Savory says but how he is interpreted. Savory talks about managing the landscape to promote different successional stages—a biodiversity of grassland, brush, woodland, rivers, and creeks. Yet ranchers tend to manage for cows and grass alone. Such management is not easy. Savory's methods require a real understanding of how complex, nonlinear, and unmechanical the world is—something we all have trouble admitting. Constant changes in weather and plant growth require constant vigilance—and a constant moving of the herd. When ranchers *increase* cow numbers and then miscalculate the timing of their grazing—that is, by letting cattle graze an area too long—the results can be disastrous.

Logistically, too, public-lands ranchers are not always in a position to easily change their management: to put up new fences, to tear out old ones, or to add stock. Any such change requires the government's approval. More emotionally, HRM is a challenge to many western traditions. A herd of cattle, for example, can be trained to respond to a whistle. In this way, one man on foot can "call up" the cows it once took three or four riders to gather. This lifeguard's technique is less labor intensive. It is also less glamorous. Traditionally, the western rancher works alone. Yet many small ranches don't have enough cows to produce the correct herd effect. The HRM solution of combining livestock with a neighbor can seem frighteningly communal. Finally, killing predators—the very animals that cows need in order to produce the "action of the thundering herd"—is a basic western reflex, as natural as putting a gun rack on the pickup.

Ultimately, the holistic rancher must become a holistic person: a communicator, an ecologist, a botanist, an accountant. The individualist must think in terms of the whole. The monoculturist must diversify. He or she must truly "kill the cowboy."

"Ranchers abuse HRM," Savory admits readily. "Many ranchers aren't even really interested in it. They just hear that they can double their production and then filter out everything else. They go on and do harm to themselves mostly."

At the very least, Allan Savory is asking the right questions. How can we restore degraded land? How can we have healthy systems of soil and water? How can humans fit into the landscape?

When Doc and Connie Hatfield went to the HRM center, they "were looking for a new way of looking at things." They particularly liked the first step of the HRM process: the formulation of a three-part goal that includes a desired quality of life, the forms of production needed to sustain that life (profit from crops, livestock, or wildlife), and the ecological landscape needed to sustain that production.

"That's the real value of HRM," Doc says. "That three-part goal. I call it a vision. Goal is too little and too hard a word for me. HRM isn't a grazing system with lots of paddocks and fences and cows going around in circles. HRM is a way of knowing what it is you want and then being creative and seeking solutions."

Savory says it more strongly. "The goal should mean more to you than anything in life. If you have certain spiritual values, those should be in the goal. If you want your children to have a college education, this should be in the goal. If you want to go sailing every summer, put it in the goal. You are not yet talking about ways of reaching your goal. *That* is a process of finding the right tools and of testing those tools with the holistic model we have. In HRM, we always assume that a solution is wrong—not right. We are always testing it."

After the Hatfields came home from Albuquerque, they tore out a fence they didn't need. They now have thirty-five pastures and use fifteen during the critical growing season of May and June. In that short time, the cattle are moved frequently, every three to seven days. The cows leave a pasture before they can take that "second bite." Then the plants grow up again. In the fall and winter, this crop of dormant grass is ready for the cows to eat at their leisure. Because the plants are not actively growing now, they are less susceptible to overgrazing. The Hatfields use their BLM lease only for winter range. During the spring and summer, they are on their own land, where it is easier to monitor and move the whistle-trained animals.

"We are always on the ground. We are always looking at the grass and the soil," Doc says. "And I can see the land responding to these cows! There's more new seedlings. There's more litter between the plants that have been tromped on, which means more nutrients and more soil cover. The grass gets more oxygen and sun after the old growth is eaten. It's richer and greener. You can see it with your own eyes."

Not long after Doc and Connie became HRM converts, the Fergusons published *Sacred Cows at the Public Trough*. Doc and Connie read the book with some irritation. In an editorial in *The Oregonian*, they asked Denzel and Nancy to visit their ranch. In fact, they invited any environmentalist to come see how well-managed livestock could actually improve an ecosystem. The Fergusons declined. But the Izaak Walton League, a national conservation group, took up the challenge.

The situation was reminiscent of Allan Savory's first visit to the ranch. The Hatfields had failed to impress *him*. Still, Doc was certain that this time would be different.

"I thought we'd get them out here, and we'd show them, and then they'd know that we were right. They'd explain that to other people, and everything would be fine." Doc laughs at himself. "That's how most ranchers are. Our response to problems is to straighten out the other guy's thinking."

Connie's concerns were rather different.

"I'm not a great cook," she confesses, "and I worried about that. I had never heard of this group. What would I feed them for lunch? What if they were vegetarians? What would they look like? Would they have little pigtails and funny shoes? I was scared to death of these people."

Connie would later describe the Izaak Walton League as "seven of the nicest older gentlemen you would ever want to meet." No pigtails, no funny shoes. At some point, she and one of her visitors were standing by a pond on the ranch. When Connie pointed out a pair of ducks that came back every year, the conservationist asked how many ducklings they produced. Well, Connie had never seen a duckling. She didn't know when these ducks nested. She didn't even know what kind of ducks they were. She just liked ducks. After a little research, she realized that cattle were invading the pond just as the birds laid their eggs. That spring, when she and Doc held off the cows a few days, a family of young cinnamon teals finally hatched.

"We had been to the Savory school," Connie says. "I had heard all about the need to consider the whole ecology of a ranch. It just hadn't clicked. It took the Izaak Walton League to show me about the ducks on my land. The environmental community has a great education to give us."

"And we have an education to give *them*," Doc finishes the equation. "Ranchers complain, you know, that the environmentalists come out on a nice day, when the sun is shining and everything looks pretty. They don't always see the reality of nature, the brutality of it, the hard times. Someone is always eating or being eaten out there. It's not kind or gentle. It's brutally beautiful!"

The Hatfields became members of the Izaak Walton League; the Izaak Walton League began to work with the Hatfields. It didn't always go smoothly. During one range tour, Doc got up and spoke his mind.

"You environmental folks are as phony as a three-dollar bill. All you do is moan and complain and file lawsuits. Show me one place where you've ever improved one acre of ground!"

There was a moment of silence.

"Why, Doc," replied one of the phony environmentalists. "I thought you understood. We don't have any land to improve or manage. The federal agencies and the ranchers do that. The only way we can make a change is by working with the laws that govern the land."

It was another turning point for Doc Hatfield. Suddenly, he could see why environmentalists so often seemed "uptight, frustrated, and angry." Suddenly, he felt sorry for them. They weren't lawyer-loving busybodies. They really cared about the land. *But they didn't own any land themselves.*

"Surely," he remarks today, because the idea strikes him still, because he still feels sorry, "improving the land by law can't be a very emotionally satisfying experience."

Insights like this led to a coalition of ranchers and environmentalists in central Oregon. Doc sees these meetings as a way of making environmentalists part of the solution.

"Ranchers have to recognize that change is occurring," Doc says. "We can maintain our ranching life and values. But we can't run cows the way we used to run them. Whatever solution we find, the environmental community has to participate. If they can be involved in the decision making, then they have ownership in the solution, and they become more than just a pain in the backside. Then, together, the environmental and the ranching community can help federal agencies make some real progress on the ground, instead of just worrying about lawsuits and funding more studies."

As usual, Connie sees another perspective. "These coalitions are giving ranchers new ways of dealing with the world. A typical meeting begins with a circle of people. Each person answers the same question. 'How do you feel about being here and what would you like to help make happen today?' I've learned that no one is truly present at a meeting until his or her voice enters the room. The question 'How do you feel?' activates the right side of the brain, the site of creativity. The second question means that something *is* going to happen."

Connie Hatfield is enthusiastic. "It's taught us to listen to other people with respect. Ranchers spend too much time in an old-boys network. They think that everyone either agrees with them or is against them. So they don't pay much attention to what you say. An important part of these meetings is that the women are personally invited. You know, in the old tradition, the man has to be the honcho, and the wife is quiet, and the son—who is about forty years old—hasn't been allowed to go to the bank yet. Five years ago, at a cattleman's association meeting, I was told to go away. They wanted me to join the Cowbelles and promote beef and give out recipes. But at our meetings now, when the men grunt and groan and can't say what they feel, the women are there to speak out and articulate their feelings. Women in general tend to be more right-brained and to understand the other person's viewpoint. We need more of that!"

Conflict resolution. Consensus. Right-brained. They may be old buzzwords to the rest of society, but in Allan Savory's experience, ranches go bankrupt because the owner does not understand these ideas. A chapter in his book *Holistic Resource Management* includes an illustration of the "hierarchically autocratic" ranch family—with a circle for "me" on top, a circle for "my wife" underneath, and two circles for "my two kids" at the bottom. Such rigid hierarchies may work for the Defense Department. But they inhibit the kind of communication and creativity needed in a modern ranch.

In another chapter, titled "Personal Growth," Savory describes "the need for a vision beyond ourselves." It is an odd echo of Denzel Ferguson.

"As I have watched the inheritance of my own children and their children deteriorate or disappear altogether, I could not stand by and do nothing. The vision I had of seeing a turnaround in my lifetime became a driving force. It has kept me going through much adversity. It has guided my pursuit of knowledge and will continue to spur whatever personal growth I manage to make for as long as I breathe."

In central Oregon, the Hatfields' ranch is a long vista of sagebrush and grass. This is a view that makes you think, really, that people evolved from birds. There are wings somewhere inside us. We can fly. This is a view that suddenly seems required.

Doc and Connie feel fortunate that they do not depend on their federal grazing lease. They could reduce their stock and stay in business. That's good, because they have strong doubts about the future of public-lands ranching.

"I don't know if it will survive," Doc says. "If you look at history, the big guy eats the little guy, and the little guy is gone. That's what's going to happen to ranchers if we try to stand and fight. Obviously we are outnumbered. But maybe we're at a time in the world when we realize that the fight is to save the world—not just to take what the other guy has got. If that's the case, then we'll keep ranching on the public lands. Because ecologically sound ranching *is* in the public's best interest."

Doc explains that early ranchers in the West naturally settled on the best areas. Thus key sections of creeks and rivers often are privately owned, with this private property interspersed throughout the national forest or BLM land. Without a public-grazing lease, these ranches no longer would be viable. Eventually they'd be sold as various small parcels.

"The urban public," Doc says, "is much better served if these large tracts are maintained as open space and as wildlife habitat. I have a suspicion that the ZX Ranch right by us, which runs twenty-thousand cows on leased federal land and which is owned by a life insurance company, is benefiting the public more than if all its private land were to be cut up, fenced, and developed. That certainly wouldn't be good for wild animals or for the health of the land."

Recently, Connie attended a meeting of the Trout Creek Mountain Working Group. This coalition began with a number of angry people. A hundred-year-old, season-long grazing program on the Trout Creek Mountains had resulted in denuded streams and creeks with only a few mature willow and aspen. One native subspecies of trout had already become a candidate for federal designation as an endangered species. Ranchers and environmentalists were about to collide. After a lot of talk, the owners of the ranch (who live in California) removed their cattle for a three-year period of rest. In 1990, a new grazing plan included changes in grazing distribution, stocking levels, and seasons of use. Fifteen miles of new fencing were planned, along with two wells, one reservoir, and fifteen miles of pipeline.

Connie remembers a moment when everything came together, when it all worked, and the flower turned to fruit.

"We asked ourselves what it was that we wanted, what was our goal? And there was an environmentalist saying, 'I need baby fish, I need intermediate fish, I need teenage fish, I need mature fish, and I need old fish.' And there was a biologist saying, 'I need baby willows and aspen, I need intermediate willows and aspen, I need teenage willows and aspen, and I need mature willows and aspen.' And the ranchers are going, 'Oh! Oh, okay, why didn't you say so before? *We thought you just wanted to get rid of the cows!*' Then the ranchers start, 'Well, we want baby ranchers, and we want teenage ranchers, and we want middle-aged ranchers, and we want older ranchers.' And everyone in that room was so surprised to learn that no one was really in opposition. We could all work together to achieve those things."

"Getting cows off doesn't help," Doc insists. "Reducing cows won't help. We just have to change our management."

"There might be *some* places where cows don't belong," Connie amends.

"Most places have ways in which management can improve the land," Doc says.

"It's a whole new way," Connie adds, "of looking at things."

As the crow flies, the Hatfields and Fergusons live within 250 miles of each other. More accurately, they inhabit different planets. They live in an Escher painting—in the constant collision of black and white.

Doc Hatfield maintains that an exclosure on Bear Creek, fenced off from grazing, doesn't look "quite as nice" as parts of the same creek grazed the HRM way.

Denzel Ferguson scoffs, "They're managing for grass. Bear Creek used to be a beaver and trout stream shaded by trees. Beaver and trout were doing fine before the cows came."

Such flat contradictions—"This is healthy!" "No, it's not!"—are all too common.

In southeastern Arizona, the Audubon Research Center has been closed to grazing for twenty-five years. Allan Savory believes that after an initial period of recovery, the Audubon land is deteriorating—its grass choking up with old growth, its natural biodiversity in decline. The researchers who live there say the opposite. They point to adjoining cattle ranches, managed with HRM, that have fewer diverse plants and wildlife. More specifically, the Audubon Research Center is rich with species that do not thrive under grazing and thus do not thrive in the West.

The experts disagree. The rest of us are confused.

Doc and Connie Hatfield are proud of the progress inherent in the Trout Creek Mountains Working Group. The BLM's new grazing plan is designed to promote the recovery of the stream area and its native wildlife. More, since key riparian habitats are privately owned in the Trout Creek Mountains, keeping this ranch alive means keeping a vast area managed as a whole ecosystem.

Denzel Ferguson looks at the same BLM plan and calls it a scam. "It pirates $40,000 of tax funds to repair public streams damaged by cows belonging to a single wealthy Californian! The grazing fees paid by this rancher do not begin to cover the costs of the water developments."

Nancy Ferguson adds, "Of course, we'll have to deal with how privately owned streams near public land are managed. We already have a lot of restrictions here in Oregon. In some cases, the government or conservation groups could buy that property. I have to wonder, too, how much public-lands ranching is preventing development. Look at Jackson or Ketchum or the Bitterroot Valley. Once prices rise high enough, ranchers tend to sell. Sometimes they slice up their private land, keep a little bit, and keep on using the federal lease!"

Black and white.

On the Hatfields' ranch, Connie insists on raising cows free of implanted hormones and antibiotics. In a unique marketing strategy, the Hatfields have joined with their neighbors to produce beef on a year-round basis for a chain of health-conscious restaurants in Japan. The Japanese guarantee a set profit that allows for the ranchers' production costs. The beef is processed by American workers before being shipped overseas. Connie remembers a dinner conversation with one of the Japanese executives. He pointed to a young mother at the table. "Do you breastfeed your baby?" he asked. After a startled moment, the woman nodded. The man explained that in Japan many women can no longer nurse because their main source of protein— fish—is too contaminated with mercury.

Connie believes she is helping mothers breastfeed their children. She believes that beef, in moderation, is a healthy food.

Denzel Ferguson says that by shipping beef to Japan we are exporting a high cholesterol diet; he points to an increase in the Japanese mortality rate.

Environmentalists worry that cattle ranching is helping to destroy South American rainforests. Livestock growers in the U.S. respond quickly: don't buy from South America.

Denzel Ferguson calls the 1992 grazing fee a ridiculous subsidy. Ranchers say that it reflects the extra time and money they must spend to graze on rugged federal land. Ranchers also believe they paid an extra cost for the grazing permit when they paid an inflated price for the ranch's private or base property.

Environmentalists point out that the contribution of public-lands ranchers to our beef supply is negligible. Only 2 percent of the total feed (forage, hay, and grain) fed to beef cows comes from the public land. Others counter that one-third of ranchers in the eleven major western states use the public land at least part of the year and that 15 percent of the nation's beef cows and 44 percent of the sheep are at least born on public-lands ranches.

"Facts!" Steve MacDonald says with some derision. "There are lots of facts. There are over five billion people in the world. Spewing out facts doesn't do any good."

Black and white.

As in many Escher paintings, as with ranchers and environmentalists, black and white can begin to intermingle. Patterns overlap and intrude. Boundaries are redefined until suddenly there is no boundary. Connie Hatfield loves to ranch because she loves animals. She loves the frisky play of calves, the groaning sound of a birthing heifer, the elk in the meadow, the eagle on the windmill. Denzel Ferguson is a zoologist. He and Nancy festoon their land with bird feeders; Nancy's favorite memory is that of a bear by the John Day River, his coat shining in the evening light.

"What we share is important."

"Stop all basic resource damage done by livestock!"

"The world isn't linear. It isn't mechanical. It only functions in wholes."

"We have a responsibility that's beyond the personal. I can't sit by and watch this land being destroyed."

"Maybe we're at a time in the world when we realize that the fight is to save the world."

"How do you feel about being here, and what would you like to make happen today?"

5. THE PHYSICS OF BEAUTY

> *The physics of beauty is one department of natural science still in the Dark Ages. Not even the manipulators of bent space have tried to solve its equations. Everybody knows, for example, that the autumn landscape in the north woods is the land, plus a red maple, plus a ruffed grouse. In terms of conventional physics, the grouse represents only a millionth of either the mass or the energy of an acre. Yet subtract the grouse, and the whole thing is dead.*
> —Aldo Leopold

IN 1919, my great-aunt Bertha married Ernest Lee, a bronc rider from the still-frontier town of Paradise, Arizona. Ernest, Dale, and Clell Lee would go on to become the famous—or infamous, depending on your viewpoint—Lee brothers, the great southwestern guides who among them killed more than 1,000 mountain lions, 1,000 black bear, 124 jaguars, and any number of bobcats, ocelots, and jaguarundis. My great-aunt spent much of her married life cooking cornbread on a wood stove in order to feed the Lee brothers' tumultuous pack of fifty hound dogs. From Dale Lee's memoirs and tape-recorded conversations, I suspect that these were men I would instinctively avoid. They were men's men: physically adept and

physically courageous. They were also racist, sexist, arrogant, and nar-
row-minded. They were on top of the world, and other men's men
sought them out to glorify and go hunting with. These men's men
had nothing but contempt for people who did not share their values;
in truth, they had a hard time understanding that other values could
even exist. You measured up to a single yardstick, or you didn't measure up at all. You were a predator or a prey.

Soon after he graduated from high school, Dale Lee and his
brothers began working as government lion hunters. As early as the
territorial days, most western counties paid bounties on livestock
predators. In 1915, the federally funded Biological Survey hired three
hundred men to kill animals on public and private land. In 1931, the
Animal Damage Control Act officially authorized the eradication,
suppression, or control of wolves, lions, coyotes, bobcats, prairie dogs,
and other creatures "injurious to agriculture and animal husbandry."

When the Lee brothers started hunting for the government,
widespread poisoning had already begun, the gray wolf was headed
for extinction in the West, and the official slogan to all ADC government trappers was an emphatic "Bring them in regardless of how!"
This, too, was a world of arrogance and glory. Wildlife existed for humanity's benefit. Methods of trapping and killing animals were brutal. The desire or means for self-evaluation did not exist. Was it wise
to blanket millions of acres of rangeland with chemicals such as
strychnine or thallium sulfate? Did coyotes and grizzly bears have a
role to play in the natural world? Did humans have the moral right
to exterminate another species? No one asked. Few of us do ask
such questions when what we are doing for a living is what we love
to do. Dale Lee watched his first mountain lion being treed by
hounds when he was thirteen years old. "And boy!" he wrote sixty
years later. "I thought that was the most beautiful sight I'd ever
seen."

The Lee brothers didn't stay with the government for long. The
work was all right, but the pay was lousy. Instead, they began to hire

out to those men and few women who would spend money for the chance to kill a cougar or jaguar. The Lee brothers could track. They could handle dogs. They could shoot, and they could skin. They could sleep outside in the cold all night and start the morning with a joke. Above all, they knew the mountain lion—its habits, likes, and dislikes, its courage and cowardices, its curved claws and big golden eyes, its very shape, smell, and texture—as few people ever would.

Steve Johnson is a professional environmentalist who grew up in Tucson, Arizona, in the 1940s and 50s. During this time, the Lee brothers continued to hunt throughout the Southwest, as well as in Central and South America. Steve Johnson never met my great-uncle. He has heard of him, of course. He even crossed paths with Dale Lee in the 1970s when both were involved in a mountain lion study done by the Arizona Game and Fish Department. Dale Lee was giving advice on how to catch a cougar. Steve Johnson was the southwestern field representative for Defenders of Wildlife, the conservation group partially funding the study. Like Dale Lee, Steve Johnson has a lifetime interest in the mountain lion. Like Dale Lee, he serves as an intermediary between wild animals and those who want to get closer to wild animals. And like Dale Lee, he has managed to make a living out of being outdoors. To pursue other similarities would be considered libelous, by both men.

The professional environmentalist is still a suspicious figure in the West—viewed even by Steven and Nena MacDonald with Quakerly jaundice. Environmentalism is an uneasily defined career choice. It usually starts with a lot of volunteer work. Later it combines altruism with a paycheck. Passion must substitute for a pension plan. Ideas are in flux. The purpose sometimes blurs.

For Steve Johnson, it happened because he went into a pet store.

The year was 1971. Steve was a twenty-five-year-old junior high school biology teacher, looking for rats to feed his snakes. Peering into one dim and smelly cage, he saw a three-foot-long alligator thrashing amid the feathers, blood, and guts of baby chickens. "Hey, that's illegal," he told his friend, the pet-store owner. "That animal is an endangered species." His friend already knew that. But what could he do when two kids beat on his door in the night and gave him the damned thing wrapped up in a blanket?

Mr. Johnson was the kind of teacher who had started an ecology club long before Earth Day. He looked at the miserably caged reptile, and he had an idea. Soon his students were collecting aluminum cans; they would send that alligator back to the Everglades! The campaign proved so successful that money was left over to donate elsewhere. The kids chose Defenders of Wildlife—perhaps they liked the name. Steve had never heard of the group before he handed it a $200 check. He began to chat with one of the board members.

Defenders of Wildlife. Steve Johnson liked the name.

It wasn't just a job. It was a great job, part-time for seven years, and full-time for another seven. From 1982 to 1989, Steve Johnson earned the approximate salary of a public-school teacher, plus an expense account. He could pick his own issues: grizzly bears in Alaska, wolves in Montana, coyotes in Texas, tortoises in Nevada. He drove about the country fighting the good fight and spent some time "on the Hill" testifying before Congress. He could pack a bag, take a flight, jump another flight, and be on the Admiralty Islands by nightfall. He knew how lucky he was.

Early on, Steve confronted the Animal Damage Control program. In one 1974 article for the *Defenders of Wildlife* magazine, he suggested that scientists at the ADC Denver Wildlife Research Center listen to the sounds of coyote pups being burned alive in their dens. "You can hear them from quite a distance," he wrote.

The poisoning of wildlife also got his attention. In the 1960s, millions of strychnine tallow pellets were scattered over the West by plane, auto, horseback, and foot. So, too, was the highly stable Compound 1080—mixed with grain to kill rodents or injected into baits of meat to kill predators. Nontarget animals often ate these baits and died. A 1963 committee, appointed by the U.S. Department of the Interior and headed by A. Starker Leopold, endorsed the use of poison but criticized ADC as indiscriminate and excessive. Leopold believed that the secondary poisoning of animals who ate rodent bodies was a serious problem. A 1971 committee was more critical still, with the result that the Environmental Protection Agency suspended the registration of the four toxicants used in predator control. In 1972, President Nixon banned their use on federal land.

Some ranchers continued to use the illegal poisons. Steve Johnson, on occasion, was the man who tracked these ranchers down. In Texas, in 1973, he stood over the hindquarters of a horse wired to a tree. Two ounces of that meat, injected with Compound 1080, was enough to kill a coyote, wolf, or dog. The method, Steve Johnson wrote, was "prophylactic, all-consuming, cheap, and easy."

"Poison," Steve Johnson says today, "is what finally exterminated the wolf and the grizzly in the Southwest. If mountain lions were more interested in scavenging dead meat than in chasing deer, they'd be gone too."

Steve talks in his kitchen, by a window that overlooks his twenty-eight acres of Sonoran Desert—saguaros like sentinels, scalloped prickly pear, buckhorn cholla twisted into old men. "In Europe, in countries that have been settled for eons, you can still see wolves. The ranchers and farmers don't like predators. But they manage around them. The cows come in at night. They use portable fences for the sheep. These ranchers would have exterminated the wolf if they could have. But there were no federal funds available. Our government chose to get into the killing business. We had the money, and we had the desire."

For environmentalists, the 1970s was a decade of progress. The 1980s seemed to reverse much of that. In 1982, President Reagan symbolically revoked the order banning chemical predacides on federal land. In December 1985, pressure from the livestock industry forced a transfer of the Animal Damage Control program, from the Department of the Interior and U.S. Fish and Wildlife Service to the U.S. Department of Agriculture. Funding for ADC increased, and predator control regained momentum.

Today, the ADC uses chemicals such as strychnine and zinc phosphide in rodent and bird control. Fumigants gas coyote and red fox pups in their dens. Sodium cyanide is placed in the M-44, an ejector device built specifically to kill coyotes. Driven into the earth, the M-44 has an odor bait or lure positioned aboveground. When the coyote pulls on the lure, a spring-activated plunger propels poison into the animal's mouth. Compound 1080 is used only in the toxic collar developed for sheep. Coyotes typically attack sheep and goats by biting them under the neck and crushing their throats. The toxic collar is attached with Velcro straps around the neck of a domestic animal; when its contents are released, it selectively kills predators caught *in flagranti*.

Other lethal methods of controlling wildlife include shooting by airplane or helicopter and quick-kill traps. Target animals caught in leg-hold, cage, or snare traps are also shot. Nontarget animals are killed or released; if they have been injured by the experience, they often are freed only to die a slower death.

Nonlethal methods of control involve frightening animals away through electronic distress sounds, propane exploders, firecrackers, lights, and water spray devices. Chemical repellents are used for birds. Lure crops and crop selection can prevent some wildlife damage. ADC also supports habitat modification and animal husbandry, such as the presence of herders, guard dogs, and fences.

When most environmentalists talk about ADC, they start with the bottom line: the body count.

In fiscal year 1990, in seventeen western states, ADC employees intentionally killed more than 809,000 animals. A partial list would include 91,158 coyotes; 8,144 skunks; 9,363 beavers; 7,065 foxes (four species); 5,933 raccoons; 3,463 opossums; 1,083 porcupines; 1,028 bobcats; 265 muskrats; 250 mountain lions; 236 black bears; 25 river otters; various rats, mice, rabbits, squirrels, cats, and dogs; and more than one-half million birds, ranging from starlings to meadowlarks. Unintentionally, ADC destroyed 5,759 nontarget animals.

Some environmentalists question the morality of killing wildlife rather than using other methods. In 1991, 90 percent of the funds spent by ADC in the West was for lethal control.

Some people think about the suffering that animals endure in traps and snares, especially when traps are not checked frequently. They invoke images of torture: denned pups stabbed repeatedly by barbed hooks, dehydrated black bears pinioned for days, live coyotes bound and mutilated to produce the "scent" required for poison and trap stations. These people have an empathetic reaction. They also have a larger concern. Why are we so unwilling to share the world?

ADC opponents see one thing clearly: this is a federally funded program that kills and maims millions of animals. The federal government is the people. The people are you and I. You and I, then, are setting traps and gassing pups. We are starving kit foxes. We are strangling bobcats. We are swooping across the Wyoming landscape in government helicopters, dealing death, playing God, endangering our souls.

That's one response to ADC, promoted by such groups as the Good Shepherd Foundation in California or the all-women Wildlife Damage Review in Arizona or the Predator Project in Montana or the New Mexicans Against ADC in Santa Fe.

Other environmentalists target the cost-efficiency of the program. In 1990, ADC field operations spent nearly $30 million. Eighty-five percent of that money went to the West, and most of that went for predator control—mainly to protect sheep from coyotes. In many of these states, the regional cost of killing coyotes, lions, and bears surpassed the losses claimed by local ranchers and farmers. Most of that cost is borne by the taxpayer. Livestock raisers are the main beneficiaries; often, only a small percentage of cattle ranchers and sheep growers benefit directly.

"Government-subsidized predator control is *really* dubious in places like national forests," says Steve Johnson, "where the price of the grazing fee has been historically kept low because of predation and other conditions. Why are public funds used to kill public wildlife on public land? Why are even private land owners subsidized by a government control program? Sheep and cattle ranches aren't failing today because of predators; they are failing because of less demand in the marketplace."

Although ADC spends a lot of money killing coyotes, the usefulness of that is in some doubt. In this century, the coyote has spread across North America, filling the niche left open by the wolf. In areas of intense control, coyotes respond by breeding earlier and increasing their litter size. In essence, we have to keep killing more coyotes just to stay even. A few people believe that intense control has only made a smart predator smarter still. Coyotes already are so intelligent that to catch "beggar animals" at National Park Service campsites in Yellowstone, rangers have to go undercover—taking off their uniforms and driving unmarked cars. The coyotes have learned to recognize the distinctive government green.

Predator expert Maurice Hornocker, who served on the 1971 committee overseeing ADC, says bluntly, "It's all been a waste of money and animals. In many cases, the best control is no control at all. Coyotes will limit their own numbers if you leave them alone."

Historically, ADC has always been the child of the western livestock industry. It still is. For the most part, ADC concentrates on what is bad for ranchers.

But Steve Johnson believes that the rancher, not the predator, is the problem. He believes that grazing on our public lands has been an ecological disaster.

"I feel a great anger when I think of what has been taken away," Steve says. "Ranchers have denied all of us the chance to see a wolf or a grizzly in the Southwest. What Thoreau calls the most glorious pages in the book of life! Someone has ripped out the grizzly bear from the heart of this country. It's not just that the big charismatic species are gone. It's not just that the government is in league with ranchers to kill wildlife. It's the loss of habitat. It's what happens when you let loose something like a cow that takes up so much space and eats so much. If insects and animals could have that forage, we'd have more of everything."

"You can't lay it all at the door of the rancher." Steve gives his punch line an extra beat. "But you can lay most of it there."

When Steve Johnson was eight years old, his family moved from Virginia to Arizona. He still remembers the car trip. His mother turned to his father in some bewilderment. "Clyde," she said in her soft southern drawl, "Clyde, these mountains are nekkid."

Later, as Steve hiked the rocky hills around Tucson, he "naturally assumed that we must grow a lot of cows here. After all, I saw cows and cow shit everywhere. But when I began to look at the figures, I was astounded. Public land in the West actually produces so little forage!" Steve says this with the kind of wail common to environmentalists who work on the grazing issue. It all seems so illogical.

"Look at what is being given up," Steve says, "for what we get."

For a while, he does not speak. I suspect he is thinking again about grizzly bears. Steve has spent a lot of time with these animals. He has spied on them in the wilderness. He has laughed at their antics and been frightened by their strength. He has felt that knowledge, thrumming through his veins and knocking in his heartbeat: *I could die now.* He has felt awe and an overwhelming sense that this was beauty. In what other way, he thinks, could we define beauty?

"Cows are dull," he says after this pause. "They are animals behind whose eyes all light has been bred out. Grizzlies are the epitome of wild places. Oh, they're messy. They smell bad. They're not manicured. They have tapeworms hanging out their anus. But, God, when you see one in a full winter coat standing on a ridge!"

Steve Johnson smiles, happy to share this memory. He is a friendly, even a gregarious man. Most of his horror stories about ranchers are prefaced with the phrase, "But, you know, I kind of liked the guy." He might even have liked the Lee brothers, at least in those moments when they proudly showed off some favorite blue hound, their faces intent in a version of love. If Steve Johnson is really going to spit bile and thunder, he saves it for that seemingly hapless, caught-in-the-middle, professorial creature—the range scientist.

"Range science," Steve hoots. "It's an oxymoron. It's a science that sprung up to justify the status quo. These are biology prostitutes. These are men who should have been in the forefront of warning ranchers, of warning people about what was happening to our soil, to our dams filling up, to our water supplies, to our wildlife habitat. Instead, these so-called scientists gave the ranchers a big bucket of sand and said, here, stick your head in here!"

Steve Johnson regrets that like most environmentalists he is often a nay-sayer. "We've come into a situation," he says, "and we want to stop the abuses of the past. At the same time, we're in the trap of playing fair. We compromise all the time. People like ranchers take in these compromises, burp, and go right on. They don't move. They don't give. Maybe we have to look at our Sir Galahad complex. Sometimes you just have to steamroll."

In 1989, Defenders of Wildlife closed their southwestern field office. The wonderful job ended. In a way, Steve Johnson was glad. Over the years, he had become convinced that grazing was the most important wildlife issue in the West. Certainly, it was *his* issue. Getting cows off the public land and getting rid of the Animal Damage Control program would be, in his mind, an "unalloyed good." As Steve pushed forward, however, he felt Defenders of Wildlife draw back. Although they continued to lobby for the reintroduction of the wolf and for control of grazing on wildlife refuges, they wanted to work more slowly within the system. They did not refer to range scientists as biology prostitutes. They were not prepared to steamroll.

It was time for Steve Johnson to be on his own. He formed a consulting firm called Native Ecosystems, with clients that include big names like the National Audubon Society and the Humane Society, as well as his former employer, Defenders of Wildlife. Working alone, Steve Johnson plots his own strategy now. He has his own plans.

We respond viscerally to a picture.

One fall afternoon, in 1989, an unhappy state wildlife official took eleven mountain lion heads out of the freezer where they were being stored, stacked them by a tree, and took a photograph. The heads are gruesome. Each has its own expression: snarling lips, a resigned sigh, eyes closed peacefully in death, eyes closed angrily against the pain. For one terrible second, it is like some horrific scene from Dante's hell. Then the viewer adjusts. These are only animals.

They are also mountain lions. They are creatures so elegant and shy that the sighting of a single one in the wild would be a memory to cherish all your life. Even longtime westerners hold fast to the day they saw a cougar's tail flick behind a rock—even that is as close as many rural westerners get. These are eleven mountain lions, all dead, dismembered, and obscurely mocked, killed by ADC hunters and trappers. This is an ugly picture. It makes the business of killing mountain lions seem ugly too.

Happily distributed by Steve Johnson, the photo got attention. It appeared in *U.S. News and World Report*. It showed up in newspapers and magazines around the country. Some people working against the ADC took heart. Animal Damage Control could go like the Berlin Wall! It only needed to be seen under the cold light of day, under the hot flash of the photographer.

Inspired, Steve Johnson began stalking ADC trappers and hunters, much as they stalk their own game. He uses a camera instead of a gun—and he has big lenses. He knows where the hunters set their traps in the forests of southeastern Arizona, where he can lay in wait, just as they do. He is eager to get another definitive picture, perhaps of a man actually killing a lion. The lion caught in steel. The death-blow.

That's one plan. The larger issue, of course, is what's at the bottom of the food chain, not at the top. The larger issue is grass and how much of it is eaten by cows every day in the dry, "nekkid" southwestern deserts. To track and pursue cows, Steve has turned to the slow-moving desert tortoise.

"I looked around cold-bloodedly for an animal that has been around for a long time and that needs practically nothing. I wanted an inoffensive animal—an herbivore that could never be accused of ripping the udders from sheep or of pecking the eyes out of a baby calf. The desert tortoise eats only about twenty pounds of forage a year, less than what one cow consumes in a day. Tortoises have been around for eons. They know how to survive. *And they're not making it.* That's how tough it is out there now. That's how little perennial grass we have left. Cows are tough too, of course. They'll eat almost anything. Unfortunately, by the time the cows go, they've taken the whole ecosystem with them."

The desert tortoise is listed as threatened in most southwestern states, except in the Sonoran Desert. (Steve Johnson is challenging the decision not to include the Sonoran population.) In California's Desert Tortoise Natural Area (sixteen thousand acres of BLM land), populations of the animal have declined 50 to 60 percent since 1970. Most biologists point to overgrazing by sheep and cattle. One study showed that after a day of grazing, sheep had taken 60 percent of the biomass of annual plants growing under creosote bushes. They reduced it by 90 percent on the second day. In effect, besides being crushed and trampled by domestic livestock, the desert tortoise was starving to death.

"Tortoises can live a hundred years," Steve says. "It's hard to see the decline. What we see are eighty-five-year-old males lumbering about looking for females. But you don't see many females, because they need more food during their pregnancies and so tend to die off. You don't see many little ones at all. In grazed areas where there's so little vegetation, ravens and other predators can spot tortoise hatchlings too easily. It always comes back to grazing. Like the spotted owl, the tortoise is an indicator species. On its back will come much of the grazing reform in the desert."

Steve points with pride to a 1991 General Accounting Office report that confirms all he has been saying for years.

The report summarizes without flair: "Current livestock grazing activity on BLM allotments in hot desert areas risks long-term environmental damage while not generating grazing fee revenues sufficient to provide for adequate management."

There are twenty million acres of BLM land in the "hot deserts," defined as the Mojave, the Sonoran, and the Chihuahuan, for which about one thousand ranchers hold grazing permits. The GAO found that "local economies do not depend on public-lands ranching for economic survival" and that many of the permittees "generate little net income from ranching." The report also notes, typically, that the BLM does not know what is happening on its own land. Forty percent of the allotments surveyed by the GAO had no livestock counts. Forty-eight percent of all allotments were not being monitored for their range conditions. Of the other 52 percent, 38 percent had not been evaluated. The report concluded that either the BLM should do its job properly (which would require a significant funding increase) or Congress should consider a halt to all grazing in hot desert areas.

Steve Johnson loves this report. He appreciates a good lawsuit. He pushes paper. He lives in a suburb. In these ways, he fits Doc Hatfield's stereotype of an environmentalist.

Still, although a few ADC opponents might be called animal ac-

tivists or even sentimentalists, Steve Johnson is neither. In the out-
skirts of Tucson, he kills packrats "regularly" because they attract the
bloodsucking conenose bug. (Like many people, his wife is allergic
to the bug's bite.) He shoots English sparrows. "They take over the
nests of the 'good birds,'" he says ironically, "the native species." He
has nothing against hunting, although he finds photography more of
a challenge. He has seen plenty of dead animals. He has probably dis-
sected a few. He knows all about the brutality of nature.

He thinks about wildlife a lot.

"They let me see things that I couldn't see otherwise. They let me
see what's real. Humans have the power to live outside the desert,
and so we don't even *know* what the desert is really like. Wildlife
shows me the limits.

"We respond to things that don't need us. From the news on TV,
we have the impression that the world turns on what happens to the
human race. Deep down, I think people are uncomfortable with that.
We make such a big deal about miniaturization and how tiny we can
make things. Look at those midges on my porch! They eat and reproduce and die. They are more amazing than anything we can ever
do. We make such a big deal about going to the moon! We were
packages delivered to the moon! A lot of us feel that way a lot of
the time. We are packages—analyzed for our buying preferences.
Wildlife is outside that. I'm glad something is.

"Time fascinates me. We see animals and their body forms and
their adaptations, and we see time. The specialists of the animal world
have lived so long in a place. It's reassuring to me, at a profound level,
that they are going to go on. There will be another world and another life after we are gone."

After we are gone?

It's a pessimism found in many environmentalists and in many
people who oppose ADC. Perhaps it particularly affects those who
deal with vanishing species.

"This is all a forestalling action," Steve warns me. "I don't think it will work. The landslide is coming. Humans are crisis oriented. It's not in our background to see slow, cumulative change. That wasn't a survival technique, and this fundamental lack isn't addressable. Before, of course, we couldn't change the earth. Now we can. And we're not equipped to do it. If we had created this system, then maybe we could tinker with it. But we don't know what we're doing, and we never did know."

This is a bleak vision to sustain. You have to hold it in your hands and hit bottom—a personal bottom—before you can rise again.

"None of us are consistent," Steve Johnson muses despondently. "We all do things in our short-term interest. I feel guilty about living out here in the desert, part of this sprawling Tucson suburbia, taking up more wild land for my personal pleasure. I should go live in town."

Now he looks distinctly depressed. He has designed and built much of this adobe house himself. In the ponderosa pine vigas, the textured walls, the brick floors, the tiled kitchen, Steve Johnson has created a sanctuary of aesthetics and grace. A small pool with floating lilies fills part of his study; the water is half in the world of people and books, half outside for the animals and birds to use. The arboreal desert outside this house is, as well, uniquely beautiful: all angles, all complexity, full of secrets. It is an exotic landscape I know from my own childhood. Even those of us born in the Sonoran Desert recognize it as rare, exquisite, and extraordinary.

Like everyone else, Steve Johnson does not want to give any of this up—not this private patch of land, not the airplane trips to Alaska, not the long car rides singing along to some beloved music, not this city in a place that clearly cannot sustain cities, not all the consumptive pleasures of our incredible century.

Well, at some point, what is there left to do but shrug and rise to the surface of hope and optimism, trailing our short-term interests behind?

"As long as you don't look at the fundamental question of 'why bother?'" Steve says more cheerfully, "then you can keep on trying. We *can* do better than what we're doing. I have dreams of what could allow some things to come back."

In these dreams, ADC is a bad memory. We have learned to share. In these dreams, we have corridors of wild habitat flowing through the country like great green rivers. We have grizzly bears in the Southwest again. We have lush stands of perennial grass. We have black-footed ferrets.

The desert tortoise finds his mate.

In these dreams, in Steve Johnson's life, the mythology of the cowboy just doesn't compute. Steve Johnson is genuinely surprised that people still *do* mythologize ranchers, that cowboys mean something in the American psyche. "I think it's because you don't know them?" Steve tries. "Or maybe it's the distinctive dress? The uniform, the costume? Is that the key? Maybe it's because they are outside most people's experience? The rosy haze of distance? I don't know. Is it because we have nothing else, I wonder?"

Steve Johnson keeps looking out his window. Past the saguaro and the buckhorn and the fuzzy cholla, a jack rabbit poses on the gravel driveway. The animal looks muscular and incongruously virile. As a cactus wren angles down, the jack crouches. The wren flies onto the rabbit, pecks, and flies off.

"I've never seen that before," Steve is intrigued. "It's obviously a routine. That bird is getting something, a tick, something. It's not just the things we don't know, you see. It's the things we don't even need to know."

Nothing moves in the desert. It is twilight, and we are all, suddenly, acutely aware of that fact. The hidden owls and Chuckwalla lizards, the packrats and kangeroo rats and kit fox underground, the peccary under a bush, the coyote in a culvert, the bobcat, the mule deer, the ironwood, the saguaro, we are all poised in twilight.

"I can't think of anything worse," Steve Johnson deliberately breaks the spell, "than a world made of just people and what people eat."

"Those of us who value public lands and the wildlife they sustain tend, therefore, to maintain vigilance against the most 'Western' symbol of all: the cowboy. In so doing, however, we must seek to base our caution upon a background of truth. This has not always been the case where issues concerning predators have been concerned."
—Harley G. Shaw

"There is no truth, there are only points of view."
—Edith Sitwell

At the 640-acre Federal Center in Denver, Canada geese stroll leisurely between demure brick buildings. The geese congregate in groups that gabble and honk before the Animal Damage Control office. These water birds do not just winter here; they are permanent members of an ecosystem that includes lots of manicured lawn, some artificial feeding, and an odd coyote or two prowling about the edge of the well-landscaped government complex. The Rocky Mountains preside over this Colorado city with its half million people. As with many western towns, wilderness and wildlife are not far away.

Guy Connolly is a wildlife biologist at ADC's Denver Wildlife Research Center. This is where most forms of control, from chemical toxicants to the new "electronic guard," are developed and tested. ADC's first and only public relations specialist, hired in 1991, describes Guy Connolly as "the closest thing we've got to a guru." Guy is a mild-mannered, low-key, bespectacled man. Raised in Montana, he is a musician, an opera lover, and a sufferer of allergies that cause him to gravitate to the city rather than the country. Guy joined the ADC in 1975 and has spent plenty of time in the field, however. He is an expert on coyote predation. For the last three years, he has been one of several workers drafting the ADC's one-inch-thick environmental impact statement. Many environmental groups decry this EIS as a justification for the status quo. Guy Connolly, of course, believes in the status quo. He believes that the Animal Damage Control program "is doing the right thing, in the right way, for the right reasons."

Steve Johnson grew up in the Southwest with a particular reverence for mountain men, grizzlies, and the romance of a more pristine past. Guy Connolly grew up in the heart of Lewis and Clark country and has his own collection of "mountain man books." Still, there is a difference. One mourns the past; the other only appreciates it. The early explorers were replaced by farmers and ranchers, and Guy Connolly finds them just as interesting. He *likes* the look of sheep and cows grazing pastorally in a green field. This, he says, is another part of his western heritage.

Simply put, Guy is anthropocentric. His own species comes first. He is not unreasonable. He would let the grizzlies have Yellowstone National Park; if human visitors get eaten on Soda Butte Creek, they knew the odds. For the most part, however, Guy sees that the rest of the wild West is no longer wild and can never be again. Human beings have entered the landscape. It is humanity's responsibility to manage the consequences.

Guy smiles at the joke the public relations specialist tells about the rancher and the preacher. The preacher looks out over the rancher's land and exclaims enthusiastically, "You and the Lord have done a wonderful job here!" The rancher gives a laconic nod. "I don't mean to be disrespectful," he replies. "But you should have seen this place when the Lord had it all alone."

In his mild-mannered way, Guy Connolly is aggrieved at the distorted view some people have of the ADC program.

For one thing, the so-called body count must be put into perspective. For example, in Colorado in 1988, ADC killed 13 black bears. Legal hunters killed 600 black bears, poachers may have killed yet another 600, and property owners and livestock growers another 300 to 600 again. Similarly, the average annual kill of mountains lions by ADC between 1979 and 1988 was 126; trappers and hunters alone killed over 1,180. ADC's average annual kill of coyotes between these years was 67,852; in an extremely conservative estimate, other people killed five times that amount. ADC may average 700 bobcats a year; the rest of America shot or trapped 59,000.

In short, a lot of wild animals are killed every day in the West—but not, for the most part, by the federal government.

Guy points out that ADC is hardly, as its critics say, "a giant federally funded killing machine." Thirty million dollars may seem like a lot of money to any one individual; it's not a lot of money for a government program that employs more than nine hundred people. In 1990, field operations required $15.80 million in federal funds, $6.34 million in cooperative funds, and $7.62 million in other funds. These last two sources include taxes levied on ranchers. Guy sees ADC as a funnel that brings together all the monies available for predator control into one accountable program. If this is a killing machine, if it is a government subsidy, then it is not a very big one.

If we are talking specifically about public lands, Guy says calmly that they account for only 10 percent of ADC's work. That number may vary from state to state. (In Arizona, it's 17 percent.) Still, ADC works predominantly on private land, at the request of private landowners. Very little public wildlife is being killed on public land with public funds.

Finally, if people want to identify a giant killing machine, they should look at the Humane Society, which strongly opposes the current ADC program. Each year, this organization is forced to euthanize some eight to fifteen *million* unwanted cats and dogs.

Like all ADC officials, Guy Connolly likes to talk about the larger scope of his program—what ADC does besides killing coyotes. In

Arizona, where Steve Johnson lives, Animal Damage Control specialists (they are no longer called government trappers) handle bird
strike problems at airports, scare ravens away from apple and pista-
chio orchards, tranquilize and remove waterfowl from swimming
pools and fisheries, kill rodents and rabbits for farmers, remove
woodpeckers that are damaging public and private buildings, help
suppress rabies, and monitor bubonic plague for the state. As elsewhere, Arizona's state director would like to expand these kinds of
activities. For now, they make up about 30 percent of his work. The
rest is in predator control.

"It's not our job to kill," Guy Connolly says. "It's our job to solve
problems. If we had practical, nonlethal ways of solving the problems
of predation on livestock, then we would use those methods. I don't
really see a time when we can eliminate all lethal methods of control. But I see a time when we rely on them less than we do now.
Husbandry and guarding dogs will become our first line of defense
even more than they are. In terms of coyotes, the biology of reproduction is the real future. Contraceptives, preventing fertilization,
chemosterilants. Unfortunately, we're a long way away from that."

Some ADC officials blame the lack of nonlethal methods on the
program's previous position in the Department of the Interior and
the U.S. Fish and Wildlife Service. Under their umbrella, ADC lan-
guished—the "black hat" of the 1970s, receiving just enough money
for maintenance but not enough for research. Environmentalists
view the ADC's 1985 transfer to the Department of Agriculture as
bad for predators; ADC sees it as just the opposite. Guy Connolly
laments a twenty-year hiatus in research on reproductive control. Today, the Denver Wildlife Research Center is just beginning those
studies again.

The actual *need* for predator control, lethal or nonlethal, is not an
issue.

"Our society doesn't deal well with death," Guy Connolly says.
"Death is a hard sell. And it should be. We want it to be. The idea

that an animal has to die because it's doing damage to someone else is not popular. But it is reality. If people don't find a legitimate solution to their problems, they'll find an illegitimate one. It's much better for wildlife that we have a government-managed, responsible, accountable program dealing with these things. If we don't have professionals out there, people will take matters into their own hands."

No one knows what really would happen if ADC did not take on the task of killing predators, but there are some disturbing possibilities. In Kansas, ADC officials are lauded by some environmentalists for their low-key program; instead of killing coyotes, a single state extension agent distributes information about trapping, guard dogs, and penning sheep under lights. In Kansas, the average annual kill of coyotes for 1979–1988 by the ADC was 1; in nearby Nebraska, the ADC kill was 1,261; in Arizona, it was 1,528. In Arizona, however, hunters and trappers annually killed 41,865 coyotes; in Nebraska, they destroyed 21,240. And in Kansas? In Kansas, they shot or trapped an average of 90,403 every year—far more than any other state in the West.

"You can get rid of ADC," Guy Connolly says, "but you can't stop people from protecting their property. It'll go underground. Toxicants are easily available. Farmers and ranchers aren't bad people. But they'll do what they have to do."

The public-relations specialist comments on a 1991 case in Wyoming. In an eighteen-month sting operation, some two dozen ranchers were caught attempting to buy banned toxins such as Compound 1080 and strychnine. Federal agents confiscated enough poison to kill every man, woman, and child in the western United States. The U.S. Fish and Wildlife Service accused the sheep ranchers of specifically targeting bald and golden eagles—the former an endangered species. The ranchers claimed that they were trying to kill not eagles (which do prey on lambs) but coyotes.

Guy Connolly doesn't condone these ranchers. But he sympathizes with them. Predation may not be the cause of the decline of ranching in this country; still, it can severely affect the livelihood of individual ranchers. According to the U.S. Department of Agriculture, in 1990 coyotes accounted for losses of about $13.6 million in sheep and lambs and $5.6 million in goats. In 1991, cattle and calf losses to all predators were valued at $41.5 million. Coyotes, the major cause of loss, accounted for $24.3 million. (Dogs were the second leading cause.)

"People like Steve Johnson may be more vocal," Guy says, "but they are probably outnumbered by others who feel that they need ADC or comparable services to stay in business. ADC is a compromise among conflicting political pressures. We receive just as much heat from interests who desire *more* wildlife damage control."

If such control is clearly necessary to Guy Connolly, it is also clearly economical. When claimed losses to ranchers are about equal to the cost of the ADC program in that region, this means that ADC is doing a good job. "If we hadn't been there," Guy exclaims, "the losses could have been ten times higher!"

"There has to be some evidence of damage," he says, "before the program is activated. We go in because there is a demonstrated wildlife problem. Then we try, as much as possible, to deal with the offending animal or the offending population. There's still some prophylactic control of coyotes—clearing them all out from a specific area. But we're moving away from that."

"Would coyotes self-regulate if they were left alone?" Guy asks rhetorically. "Of course they would. But people don't leave them alone. It's wishful thinking to believe otherwise. Also, coyotes might not self-regulate to the point where they didn't cause damage. Nature won't resolve the problem the way man wants it to be resolved."

Guy returns to the idea of reproductive inhibitors. Coyotes, in particular, kill more sheep during the spring, when they have pups to feed. Fewer pups means less predation. "We *know* that prophylactic control just stimulates reproduction," Guy says. "The more nonlethal our methods are, the more biologically sound they are—because they are not removing animals from the population."

Steve Johnson would agree. Indeed, if you were to put these two in a room together, they might agree on a number of things. "But, you know," Steve Johnson might conclude, "I kind of liked the guy." It seems, even, that these men could come to a truce concerning the Animal Damage Control program.

That may be more wishful thinking.

Steve Johnson is not opposed to control or to wildlife management or to accountability. He is opposed to the "disproportionate stranglehold" that livestock growers have on the West. The ADC spends most of its energy supporting an industry that Steve Johnson thinks is inherently harmful to western wildlife. More, the ADC *trusts* ranchers—and Steve Johnson does not.

"ADC is called in," Guy Connolly assures me, "because the rancher has already tried everything in his bag of tricks. If there were a nonlethal method of control available, the problem wouldn't have come to our attention. We don't work on a place where the rancher is not doing everything he knows of in terms of good management."

Huh? Steve Johnson might reply.

Guy Connolly insists that ranchers *are* changing. They are better informed. They read. They experiment. A few, such as Doc and Connie Hatfield, manipulate their cattle's breeding cycle so that calves are born at a time when other prey are plentiful. About one-third of western ranchers use lambing sheds instead of having sheep birth on the open range. Guard dogs, guard burros, and even guard llamas are at least receiving publicity. Guy Connolly talks of a certain "hang-dog" look that ranchers have when forced to call in ADC; it's a sign of failure to them.

Guy Connolly also says that ADC is changing—at a rapid pace. "The perception of ADC is historical," Guy complains. "People accuse us of things that we did twenty or thirty years ago. No one is going to say now that we should eliminate the wolf. Our employees are not sadistic killers. They are no longer graded on how many bodies they 'bring in.' We are not 'out of control.' We have twenty-six different regulations on how to use the M-44 alone. We are always looking for better methods."

Guy holds up the hefty environmental impact statement. "This last EIS was for the fiscal year of 1988, and even as we worked on it, we questioned whether our current program was being fairly represented. We are moving more and more away from traditional lethal control."

Steve Johnson's response is cynical. In fact, the 1990 General Accounting Office's report on ADC notes that "although the ADC policy manual states that nonlethal methods will be given first consideration . . . little evidence exists of state ADC program personnel employing such methods."

Alarmingly, in the case against Wyoming ranchers, much of the poison confiscated was seized at the Wyoming's Department of Agriculture's Predator Control Lab, with a state predator control official selling the poison. This was not ADC, but ADC prides itself on working hand in hand with state departments and state agents. The investigation itself had to be rigorously shielded from political influence. Top Interior Department officials in Washington did not know about the sting until hours or days before the first search warrants were used; the U.S. Fish and Wildlife Service feared that details might otherwise leak out on Capitol Hill and get back to the sheep ranchers.

This last precaution points to the hold that ranchers have on western politicians and on agencies like ADC. In 1992, the secretary of agriculture's National Animal Damage Control Advisory Committee consisted of eighteen members—two scientists, eight members directly linked to livestock production, and eight others linked to commodity interests.

Steve Johnson believes he has good reason to be suspicious. Sitting in his office, Guy Connolly is both sincere and persuasive. But no one knows exactly what is happening out in the field. Even if ADC wanted to change, would the livestock industry let it?

Fundamentally, it comes down to these feelings of suspicion, trust, and mistrust. It comes down to intuition and prejudice. It has to, because for many questions, the answers simply aren't available.

How, for example, is wildlife really faring in the West? The General Accounting Office concludes, with some chagrin, that the federal government doesn't know. The high numbers of animals killed every year could mean that we have a lot of animals out there to kill. Or it could mean that we are not going to have many animals in the future.

People like Guy Connolly and Steve Johnson have very different visions.

As an ADC biologist, Guy is concerned with the maintenance and survival of entire populations. The GAO report clearly says that the ADC program does not seriously affect predator numbers. The animals that ADC does kill tend to be the ones that thrive in the presence of humanity—that's *why* they are being killed. Coyotes, certainly, are in no danger of extinction, nor is the mountain lion. (In urban areas like Denver, an excess of mountain lions is coming down into the streets, attacking domestic dogs as well as joggers and children.) In Guy Connolly's West, wildlife is doing just fine. Deer are everywhere. Elk are increasing. Game animals, overall, are in better shape than they've been in the last fifty years. The return of the bald eagle is an incredible success story! When Guy Connolly goes back to hunt ducks on the Yellowstone River, he sees more waterfowl than he ever saw as a boy. "We've had some good luck in preserving habitat," he enthuses. "There's been some wonderful stewardship of the West."

Steve Johnson wonders. Some 100,000 bald eagles once lived in the continental United States. Today, about 2,600 nesting pairs survive, with less than 10,000 birds altogether. Some federal officials believe that 2,000 to 3,000 bald eagles are poisoned each spring by ranchers. Is that a success story? As for mountain lions, who really knows how many there are? Certainly, when a rancher kills thirteen lions on a single grazing allotment in the Coronado National Forest, local populations *are* being affected. Local biodiversity is diminished.

Concerning other populations of wildlife, a 1990 GAO report was not optimistic. The GAO concluded that while game species seem to be recovering from historical lows, many others were not "faring as well in part because of public lands habitat deterioration."

"There is," the GAO tolled, "reason for concern."

People like Guy and people like Steve see a different past, a different present, and a different future.

"In my business, we have to look ahead a hundred years," says the ADC state director in Arizona. "The demand for agricultural products and for all natural resources is only going to increase. ADC's role is to make the interface between humans and wildlife workable. Someday if people have to choose between food and wildlife, they will choose food. We'll *lose* wildlife if we don't control it."

This man believes in technology. He believes that if we learn enough, research enough, and plan enough—we can do it right. He's willing to take on that responsibility. To his credit, he is grounded in a sense of responsibility.

"We have met the enemy," the ADC state director says, "and he is us. Eventually there must be changes in how we consume resources. Eventually we must deal with our exploding population. But you can't force those changes down people's throats. If you push too far, the pendulum will swing back. There will be a backlash against wildlife."

For the Arizona state director and for Guy Connolly, ADC is a symbol of hope. We control wildlife to keep wildlife.

For Steve Johnson and for others, ADC is a symbol of destruction. It is another version of hunter Dale Lee, of arrogance and casual brutality, of an old-boy network (scratch my back, I'll kill your mountain lion), and of a future that blindly repeats the mistakes of the past. In this future, we have not learned anything about the limitations of our flaunted technology. We are spiritually bereft, struggling to control with guns and traps and poison a natural world that, in truth, is our home and our body and our womb. In this future, wildlife is lost not because of some hypothetical backlash but because we never learned to live with wildlife.

In this future, we show a singular lack of intelligence. Steve Johnson reminds me that to produce 1 kilogram of beef in the United States requires 4.8 kilograms of grain and 3,000 liters of water. The demand for more agriculture is not, necessarily, best served by more livestock.

Guy Connolly would argue this point. Those figures probably apply to cows fattened in feedlots for at least the last four months of life. But range cattle *could* be marketed so as to require much less grain. In essence, grass-eating ruminants convert into human food a renewable resource that is unpalatable to humans; people have been successfully exploiting this ability for thousands of years. Realistically, we may cut down on beef in our diet, but we won't eliminate it. In terms of our health—in terms of the animal's well-being—wouldn't we rather have cows on the range than in a factory farm?

Blink. The Animal Damage Control program comes into focus. Blink. It's gone again.

One thing is clear: Guy Connolly is not Dale Lee.

Who was Dale Lee anyway? I once met a public-lands rancher in southeastern Arizona who had all the physiognomy and psychology of the cowboy myth. He was tall, rangy, weathered, courtly, thoughtful, and self-deprecating. He said grace before we ate lunch. Unlike Denzel Ferguson's version of the ignorant rancher, this man knew his grassland ecology, his sacaton from his side-oats. He had learned about the particulars of his ranch from his father and from his grandfather, and they had managed, throughout the years, to take good care of the land. I trusted this man intuitively. He was a good person. I could tell.

"The Lee brothers," he said slowly. "Yes, I knew them. Fine folk. They were fine, fine folk."

Perhaps they were.

This rancher was about to lead a mountain lion hunt. Such hunts were the extra income he needed if he was not going to abuse the public lands he ranched. Like Dale Lee, he has an intimacy with the animals he kills. He knows the mountain lion far better than I do. I am not prepared, yet, to say that his relationship is wrong.

The ADC state director in Arizona tells of a grenade thrown in his office's parking lot. In the last three years, he has received a number of death threats by phone and mail, presumably from radical environmentalists. He struggles to be fair.

"I do need a counterbalance to the cattleman's viewpoint," he says. "I need people to help us get more funding for research and nonlethal techniques. We're frustrated here. We're limited by what our technology allows us to do. I need help from the environmentalists. But it needs to be constructive."

"We'd like a lot of alternatives that we don't have," says Guy Connolly, "but we have to live in the real world. If the current ADC program vanished, I think most of its work would be assumed by state and local programs. The most significant change would be loss of the national oversight that exists today. In addition, state and local programs would not have to comply with the National Environmental Policy Act. In this scenario, opponents like Steve Johnson would have to deal with dozens of programs, not just one."

"These people who want to get rid of the ADC simply don't understand us," says the Arizona state director. "And they don't understand what would happen without us."

"We *can* do better than what we're doing," Steve Johnson insists.

We know that, at least, for sure.

"I called this exchange in which the animals appear to lock eyes and make a decision the conversation of death. It is a ceremonial exchange, the flesh of the hunted in exchange for respect for its spirit. In this way both animals, not the predator alone, choose for the encounter to end in death. There is, at least, a sacred order in this. There is nobility. And it is something that happens only between the wolf and his major prey species. It produces, for the wolf, sacred meat. Imagine a cow in the place of the moose or the white-tailed deer. The conversation of death falters noticeably with domestic stock. They have had the conversation of death bred out of them; they do not know how to encounter wolves."
—Barry Lopez

Not everyone is impressed when the wolf enters the room. The teachers are busy watching their students, keeping them quiet, worrying about loud noises. Some of the children are aware that this wolf, after all, has a name: Shaman. This is a named wolf on a leash brought to this school in a van. This is a named, tamed wolf, surely, really, not much more than a dog.

The wolf enters the room. His nails scrabble on the hard floor. He strains at the leash, lunging, eager, curious, excited, only slightly frantic. He has done this sort of thing since he was two weeks old. He has faced many rooms of people, and he will allow himself now to be touched and petted. He will allow his friends Pamela Brown and Kent Weber to parade him before a line of human faces and human scent. He is not a dog, and there are those in the room who know this immediately—who feel immediately the charge of knowledge like a luminous coil circling up their spine. This wolf is three times as strong as any dog his size. His head is larger to hold his larger brain; his jaws have twice the crushing power of a German shepherd; his eyes are set at a different angle; his legs are longer and more spindly; his paws are huge. This particular Northern Rocky Mountain timber wolf weighs about one hundred pounds and has a black coat that is highlighted, subtly, to enhance signals that he uses in communication with other wolves. This is an animal born and raised in captivity that no one could say is wild. Still, he carries within him, in those yellow eyes and in that powerful body, all the genes of wildness and all the potential.

Pamela has prepared the audience. "Shaman will decide what to do," she tells them. "It's up to you how long he stays in here. If you are quiet and respectful, you can get to know him. If he is frightened, he'll drag Kent back out of the room."

In this auditorium, full of Pueblo Indian children of all ages, the students have a good sense of what it means to be quiet. The wolf brushes by a group of adolescent boys. They look at each other in obvious delight. The wolf returns to them, and they run their hands through his fur. Then they smell their hands—wolf smell. Shaman moves on to more children. More hands reach out to touch his luxuriant, miraculous coat. Like a wolverine's fur, Shaman's won't collect ice when he breathes against it in cold weather. The long outer guard hairs shed moisture and keep the dense underfur dry; by placing his muzzle and nose between his rear legs and wrapping his face in his tail, Shaman could sleep comfortably in the open at forty degrees below zero.

As the wolf moves about the room, some of the children look apprehensive. Wolves have forty-two teeth adapted to seize, tear, and crush. The incisors strip shreds of meat from bone. The upper premolar and a lower molar act like pruning shears to slice and snip through tough connective tissues and tendons. Wolves have tremendous upper-body strength, the better for bringing down large prey such as deer and elk. "Shaman is not a pet," Pamela has told this group again and again throughout the presentation. "Wolves and wolf hybrids do not make good pets."

A few of the children are upset by a movie they have just seen in which a wolf was shot by government trappers. One little girl frowns fiercely to keep from crying. The tendency to anthropomorphize animals makes sense when it comes to wolves. "Socially, we are a lot like wolves," Pam tells the children. "That's why dogs are our most popular pet, because they fit well into the human social structure." Wolves survive through group cooperation. The paramilitary description of a wolf pack, with its emphasis on dominance and hierarchy, is misleading. Wolves have complex and dynamic systems of interaction, family life, and entertainment. They sing. They celebrate. They love to play. In the wild, they romp with their pups and have games of tag. They hide behind bushes and jump out to scare each other. By necessity, they are alert and curious and intensely in the present. They remind us of how we must have been when we, too, hunted and gathered as a tribal society. For a child, the connection to wolves can be quite strong and personal. Naturally, children cry when they see wolves die.

Whatever their emotion—frightened, or sad, or delighted—by now everyone in the room is focused on Shaman. As the wolf follows his nose and interests, Pamela Brown throws out little comments. "Shaman is a ham," she says cheerfully to the school principal. "He knows how to work his audience." For a while Shaman goes under a table, threatening to bring down its cloth cover. Patiently, Kent Weber holds the leash. Shaman sniffs at a microphone. He stops beside a woman teacher.

"One of my favorite things about wolves," Pam says, "is that they are silent. They howl and they occasionally bark, but their vocalization is not as varied, say, as a coyote's. Wolves use body language instead. They use psychic communication. That's another thing that wolves have to teach us. You know almost everyone has had some kind of psychic experience. Usually, it's with your mother or your dog! Well, wolves use this special communication all the time, over many miles.

"Wolves are very timid," Pam reminds one boy who is giggling with a friend. "They are more scared of men than women. Most men are just too loud and scary and big. That's why wolves are rarely seen in the wild. Wolves are smart, too. They can't be trained to be a guard dog. At the first sign of trouble, they are the first to run!"

"Like people, wolves have their own personalities," Pam turns to another child. "Shaman is here with you today because he is more sociable and passive than other wolves. I have to warn you about one thing, though. Shaman likes bubblegum. So be careful. Don't show him that you have any."

"Have you ever been bitten?" a girl asks.

"Oh yeah," Pam says and rolls up her sleeve. "The only time I ever got bit was because of my own temper. People today have a lot of anger. But living with wolves has taught me to control my anger, to tone down my act. The wolf gave me plenty of warning. He growled and showed me that he didn't like what I was doing. I didn't pay enough attention. You can't have a big ego or try to throw your weight around with wolves. That doesn't work."

The children stare at the scar on Pam's forearm.

"Afterwards," Pam smiles, "that wolf would pull the bandage off my arm and gently lick the wound clean. We were always the best of friends."

At other school programs, and at shows for adults in churches and public halls, Pamela Brown and Kent Weber talk about wolves, bring in Shaman, show him off, and talk again after Shaman has returned to the van. The point being made is subtle. This is not a traveling zoo.

"What is happening to wolves," Pamela says, "is symbolic of what is happening to our environment. This program is about respect for all life. We are all connected in this world. Whatever happens to

Brother or Sister Wolf will happen to us. We all have a place in the circle of nature."

Pam reminds her audience of America's early, pathological efforts to exterminate wolves. Today, Minnesota is the only state in the lower forty-eight that did not eradicate this species. Wisconsin is slowly and naturally being repopulated, as are Montana and Idaho. There are between 6,000 and 7,000 wolves in Alaska and as many as 50,000 in Canada. (In both areas, wolves are legally hunted and killed by helicopter and plane.) Italy may have 300 wolves and Poland has jumped to 1,000. No one knows what the population is worldwide.

Pamela Brown did not grow up in Canada or Alaska or in any place that had wolves. She grew up in the rural, northwest corner of New York. Although she spends a lot of time in schoolrooms now, she never liked school as a child and dropped out at the age of sixteen. She felt too confined. In the 1960s and 1970s, she lived in Manhattan, where she raised her daughter and worked in offices for lawyers and advertising agencies. "That," she says, "was a tremendous education!" By 1978, she was sharing a house in Connecticut with "other alternative people" and looking for something special to do with her life. One day, John Harris, who had been traveling about the country for nine years doing wolf education programs, came to visit with a wolf named Slick. There was an immediate rapport among the three of them: Pam, John, and Slick.

John Harris was raised in his family's wrecking yard in Hayward, California, where he rode with the Hell's Angels and became involved in the Native American movement. His work with wolves was eventually featured in national magazines and talk shows. John believed firmly that wolf education should not be entangled with politics, government grants, or big environmental organizations. He believed that teaching people about wolves required an unusual kind of commitment. It required a sense of freedom and honesty and directness. It had to be grassroots. It had to be uncorrupted. He and Pam were partners for seven years that included, in Pam's words, "thousands of programs, the political assassination of Slick, two trials, ongoing political harassment, and three more program wolves."

"You're the one," John Harris would say to Pamela Brown. "You're the one who can carry this on."

When John died in 1985, Pam moved to Santa Fe, New Mexico. At first, she carried on with a slide show instead of a wolf. Then she heard of a young man in Colorado who had inadvertently formed a wolf sanctuary; at that time, Mission Wolf had five wolves, abandoned by their owners, which Kent Weber kept in a two-acre enclosed pen. Kent wanted to get involved in wolf education. "If you're serious," Pam said sternly, "I'll book us a trip. But you'll need a van, and it'll have to have a strong cage in the back, and it'll have to be built a certain way, and it'll have to be dependable."

When Kent and his wife pulled up to Pam's house in four months, they had the van. An adult wolf named Lucas and a puppy called Shaman, as well as two big dogs, sat in the back.

For Pamela Brown, the future of the wolf lies in those hands that reach out to touch Shaman's fur. "I like teaching children," she says. "I like teenagers. I like wacky, off-the-wall people."

Traveling with a wolf also is a kick. "We modern humans are living at half-volume," Pam says. "We're in an apathetic, caged, domesticated state. But we can be turned up. When that wolf comes into the room, all the senses are alert. When you live around wolves, you get hooked on that kind of elevated state of consciousness. It's exhausting, of course. Because you also have to pay attention to people and to their interactions with the wolf. People have no sense of how to move or behave with a wild animal. I've seen parents walk up and offer their babies. This happens regularly!"

At least once a year, Pamela goes back east to family and friends. She takes her wolf program with her—the new video she helped produce or a documentary from the Canadian Film Board—traveling from upstate New York down to the Florida coastline. These shows are different from the ones she does in the West, where cowboys heckle her from the audience and ranchers try to stop her at the schoolroom door. In my own town of Silver City, when a representative from the New Mexico Livestock Association protested wolf education at a school board meeting, the superintendent promptly cancelled Pam's program. Later Pam herself cancelled all appearances in southern New Mexico because she feared for Shaman's life. Such things rarely happen in New York or Florida. Perhaps this is why Pam always returns to the West. The tension is here. The anger is here. The future will be decided here.

"I've done hundreds of shows in New Mexico and Arizona and Colorado and Texas," Pam says. "I don't mind when ranchers or other people try to intimidate me. That bounces right off. I keep in mind that I'm a grandmother. And my grandchildren will inherit this mess. I talk to my audience about personal responsibility. If you are going to let livestock loose on the public land, then you should do the job right. If sheep and cattle are guarded by herders or dogs, then depredations are rare.

"Wolf keeps us sharp. Wolf teaches us about the wisdom of natural selection. Without wolf, there's overpopulation of deer and rodents, overgrazing, and the eventual degradation of our grandchildren's land. For a long time now, humans have had this wonderful affair with the intellect. Now we have to get back into balance with nature. We have to restore some kind of harmony."

In the 1980s, it was Pam Brown who laid the groundwork for the struggle to reintroduce the most vulnerable of all wolf subspecies—the Mexican wolf. Wolves were never numerous in the Southwest; the historic carrying capacity of New Mexico was probably only about 1,500 animals. Under a vigorous predator control program, two southwestern subspecies quickly became extinct. In the United States, the last wild example of the third, *Canis lupus baileyi,* was killed in 1970—although a small population of *lobos* continued to

exist in Mexico. In 1976, the Mexican wolf was listed under the Endangered Species Act, perhaps one of the most amazing pieces of
legislation in the history of the world. The act mandates that an endangered species be not only protected but recovered as well. Accordingly, by 1980, six Mexican wolves were removed from the
Sierra Madre of Mexico and placed in a breeding program. In 1982,
the U.S. Fish and Wildlife Service, the agency in charge of conserv-
ing endangered species, approved the Mexican Wolf Recovery Plan.
At that time, some fifty wolves were thought to remain in central
Mexico, with a handful of animals in captivity.

The purpose of the recovery plan was to reestablish a viable, self-
sustaining population of at least one hundred Mexican wolves
within their historic range. That's what the report said. That's what
the law said. That's what everyone, officially, said was going to
happen.

In truth, when money to expand the breeding program was denied, the leader of the Mexican Wolf Recovery Team wrote to her
colleagues: "As I understand it, limited FWS funds had to be committed to other projects because FWS sees no real hope for restoration of Mexican wolves anywhere in the wild."

Three years later, in 1986, the regional director of the Fish and
Wildlife Service finally wrote game officials in Arizona, Texas, and
New Mexico in search of a reintroduction site. Arizona noted
blandly the problem of predation on livestock; Arizona had no sites
to offer. Texas said that the Big Bend National Park and Guadalupe
Mountains were suitable—although Texas had a law that made wolf
reintroduction illegal. New Mexico suggested one site only, the
White Sands Missile Range.

By now, most of the wild population of wolves in Mexico had
been killed off, and there were less than thirty Mexican wolves in
captive breeding pens.

A study of the four-thousand-square-mile missile range—essen-
tially closed to public access and completely closed to cattle or

sheep—was funded. The Fish and Wildlife Service assured the military that these endangered wolves would be an experimental population, legally killed if they wandered off the range or interfered with the defense of our country. Submitted in February 1988, the study concluded that the missile range could support some thirty-two Mexican wolves. Five months before that, however, the general at White Sands had already made up his mind. The decision against reintroduction probably was based on the military's reluctance to annoy the state's ranching community.

The regional director of the Fish and Wildlife Service issued this statement: "We have no sites. The wolf reintroduction program, as of now, is terminated."

Carol Martingdale was an anthropology student at the University of New Mexico. Years ago, she had run a farm of one hundred hogs and sixty goats in southern California. She had learned to live with predators and to respect them. Carol's premise is simple. "Wolves have a right to be here too." When she read that the Mexican wolf had been bureaucratically dumped, left to slowly die out in zoos and breeding pens—another extinction, another sputtered flame—she was shocked. She had one friend with a computer and one who did artwork. She spent a day tacking up fliers around the UNM campus. They were not radical. "Write to your congressman," Carol urged. "Help save the *lobo.*"

Sue Larson, a local veterinarian, saw the flier. As a child, Sue had been horrified by road kills; long car drives with her parents were inordinately depressing. In veterinary school, she was called a "humaniatic" by the other students, many of whom came from ranching backgrounds and saw animals in a more utilitarian light. Sue deprecates her emotional bond with other species, as she has been taught to do. "I know it sounds corny," she confesses and mimics a smarmy tone. "I became a vet because I *really liked* animals." When Sue speaks of wolves, however, she makes a point of being unsentimental. Wolves *will* start eating their prey before it is properly dead.

Wounded or vulnerable wolves may be killed by their own pack. Parent wolves eat puppies that act diseased or strange.

"You have to have some romance about wolves to get involved in reintroduction," Sue concedes. "But on a practical level, you can't afford it."

Sue took a flier home and contacted Carol. So did others. Surprisingly soon, the Mexican Wolf Coalition held its first meeting. It was, by all accounts, an odd mix. There were biocentrics and anthropocentrics. There were representatives from Greenpeace and from the federal government, from the Audubon Society and from Earth First! For the next three years, this citizen's action group worked together to marshal public support for the Mexican wolf. Many of these people had seen Pam Brown's program. They all built on what she had done. In New Mexico, they confirmed what other national polls already showed: overwhelmingly, most Americans like the idea of wild wolves. At basketball games and meetings, using Sierra Club and Audubon mailing lists, the coalition passed around a petition. Do you want the *lobo* back? Some twenty-two thousand New Mexicans said yes.

Yes.

That was nice, but it wasn't really news. It didn't light a fire under the Fish and Wildlife Service. It didn't impress the Defense Department at all.

Lori Fish (who has asked that her real name not be used) and Dan Moore belonged to the Mexican Wolf Coalition. They also had ties to Earth First! They were then in their twenties, younger than most of the other coalition members. Longtime colleagues, they saw themselves as warriors—warriors and clowns. They are, today, in an awkward position. Their lives stretch ahead, middle-class Anglo-American lives, a road to success that is straight and paved and almost without speed limit. Their lives are full of opportunities and choices. Yet both Lori and Dan feel that almost anything they might choose would be a form of betrayal. They see, as clearly as Steve Johnson or the Arizona state director of ADC, how consumerism and overpopulation drive the consumption of natural resources. They see the train wreck. They stand at a street corner and look around at the cacophony of metal and plastic and energy use, and they suddenly think, "Wow. How can we keep this up? How can we sustain this? *This is crazy.*"

The generation that came of age in the 1960s saw a flawed culture and tried, optimistically, to change that culture. The generation that came of age in the 1980s saw a flawed species, the entire human race out of control. How do you change that?

From such insight, Lori Fish and Dan Moore make the kind of decisions that Steve Johnson made twenty years ago, when decisions were easier. Will Lori have children? She says no. Will Dan? He talks in circles. (In part, he is being polite; he is, after all, talking to me—a mother.) Do they use a car? Lori lives on a piece of land that has no running water or electricity or telephone, in a remote county where the population averages one person per square mile. She owns a car so that she can go to meetings like those held by the Mexican Wolf Coalition. Dan lives in Albuquerque and rides his bicycle. How do they make a living? Lori shrugs. She doesn't need much money. Dan has an odd assortment of part-time jobs, none of which completely please him. He mutters. What is right livelihood? What is right action?

How do they decide, I wonder, when to buy a new pair of shoes? How old must shoes get before they can be thrown away? What consumer pleasures are allowed? Can they eat at McDonald's? Can they go to a movie? (The cost of the most popular movie playing now would probably be enough to reintroduce the Mexican wolf and run the program—at about $400,000 a year—well into the twenty-first century. In America, the cost of reintroduction is something of a red herring.)

"All these diversions and temptations," Dan sighs. He is not completely serious. He is an intelligent, funny guy who finds refuge in self-mockery. "And the positive reinforcement is always in the wrong direction! It's a struggle to keep doing the right thing, to keep from being sucked back into the wrong thing."

"You gotta keep fighting," Lori says. "If you don't keep fighting, it'll just get worse. You gotta fight. And you gotta have a sense of humor."

At the beginning of 1990, both Dan and Lori believed that the Mexican Wolf Coalition was seriously lacking in these two qualities—in gumption and in humor. The conservative element in the coalition seemed to be in control, and the Mexican wolf was not much better off as a result. Dan and Lori were told to "wait, just wait." They were told that the general at White Sands was about to retire, that there were competing environmental agendas, that deals were being made behind the scenes. Defenders of Wildlife started its compensation fund for ranchers; the money would be paid directly to livestock owners suffering losses from reintroduced wolves. Everywhere, wolf advocates were trying hard to be reasonable. It was the Sir Galahad complex.

Lori went north to Montana to talk with the more radical Wolf Action Group. Dan went to Santa Fe to talk with Pamela Brown. They both came back feeling righteously litigious. In that mood, they decided to sue the secretary of the interior and the secretary of defense for failure to enforce the Endangered Species Act. (Under the act, all federal agencies are required to cooperate in carrying out endangered species recovery programs.) They would force the government to support its own policy. They would take action because "We are the only ones with enough balls or, in my case, enough ovaries to go for it," said Lori Fish. "It's an example of grassroots volunteers leading the way."

Not everyone felt so ballsy. At a meeting of the Mexican Wolf Coalition, an environmental lawyer gave them the worst-case scenario. If they pursued this suit and lost, they might damage—even ruin!—the Endangered Species Act. It was a dangerous precedent. The Mexican Wolf Coalition got nervous. Dan and Lori got mad.

"What good is a law if you can't use it?" Lori asks. "If we can't enforce the Endangered Species Act, then we've already lost it."

On their own, Dan and Lori hired another lawyer and, with his help, got the Sierra Club, Environmental Defense Fund, National Audubon Society, and Wilderness Society involved. In the end, all these organizations, as well as the Mexican Wolf Coalition, joined the lawsuit. (The president of the coalition resigned.) Dan Moore and his friends took the petitions with their twenty-two thousand signatures and strung them on a ribbon thirty yards long. They presented this to the regional director of the Fish and Wildlife Service. It was a photo opportunity. It was a gift to newspaper writers who could employ puns such as "Wolf Advocates Howl in Protest!"

Later that summer, Dan, Lori, and forty other demonstrators literally howled in front of the downtown federal building in Albuquerque, throwing their heads back and cupping hands around their mouths for the sake of projection. (It is an absorbing fact that humans can mimic the sound of howling wolves enough so that wolves respond with curiosity and interest. Some hunters use this method to lure wolves to their deaths.) Lori Fish dressed as a black-robed judge, for the federal agencies at that time were trying to have the lawsuit dismissed by a U.S. district court. "Tell it to the judge!" the crowd kept chanting. "Out of the zoo in '92!"

The media loved it. "You don't have to be very outrageous in this society to be outrageous," Lori notes. "A few wolf howls. It doesn't mean much politically. But it keeps our spirits up."

Publicity, headlines, anger, wolf howls—a lawsuit! The Fish and Wildlife Service began to backpedal, and the Defense Department too cried out that they were, by gosh, they *were* considering wolf reintroduction at White Sands. The Endangered Species Act was being held up like a golden shield, a chalice, the grail itself—and the magic was working. The best case scenario was coming down the pipe.

During this time, Pamela Brown spent a day with the schoolchildren at the White Sands Missile Range. Not one was aware of the Mexican Wolf Recovery Program.

By 1992, Mexican wolves were not out of the zoo. But, as everyone agrees now, the lawsuit had been successful. Tumultuous public meetings were held ("I thought I was at a rodeo," Dan remembers), and the Fish and Wildlife Service began preparing an environmental impact statement for reintroduction of the Mexican wolf in the Southwest. Arizona found four sites to evaluate. Texas began studying Big Bend National Park. In 1993, environmental organizations agreed to dismiss the lawsuit if the government continued forward with the process of reintroduction.

Suddenly, however, breeding was the problem. There weren't enough new litters to increase the captive wolf population, and biologists wanted a pool of seventy-five to one hundred wolves before they would let any loose. Today, the release of an experimental group of Mexican wolves, either at White Sands or in the Blue Range of eastern Arizona, is not expected until at least 1995. Even that will not happen if more funds are not made available.

Carol Martingdale and Sue Larson and Lori Fish and Dan Moore are watching. They want to see the end of the race. They are also ready to pursue other interests. Carol is concerned with Native American rights; she talks about human diversity. "Why do we all have to be alike?" she wonders. "Bo-ring!" Like Steve MacDonald, Lori Fish is promoting land health in the national forests that make up her own backyard. Sue Larson would like to help other endangered species, less glamorous ones perhaps. Dan Moore now works with the Citizens for Alternatives to Radioactive Dumping; he is also a paralegal for two women lawyers who take on cases in police abuse, prison rights violations, and sexual harassment.

I ask them, each one, why they have fought so hard to help reintroduce the Mexican wolf. As they well know, there are many, perhaps more important environmental causes. The wolf, after all, is not an endangered species worldwide. And the Mexican wolf, although truly endangered, is only a subspecies. More subtly, the recovery plan for the Mexican wolf is extremely high tech. It is frankly repugnant. Before the animals are let loose, radioactive discs will be surgically placed in their stomachs so that orbiting satellites can track their scat. The released wolves will then be radio-collared, monitored, and controlled—that is, killed—if they misbehave. Any pups born in the wild also will be caught, measured, deparasitized, radio-collared, and fitted up with radioactive dye. This is humanity at its busiest. This is the irony of space satellites beaming in on a single pack of wolves living a carefully managed "life in the wild" on a military missile range.

There are those who wonder if this is what the modern environmentalist should be doing.

Dan just looks at me. *Who is this woman?*

"Oh man, the big existential question," he sighs. "You don't want to ask anything hard, do you? Well . . . " he gathers steam, "the way I see it is that from 1987 on, we got a 911 emergency call. If we hadn't responded, nothing would have happened. The Mexican wolf would have simply gone off the face of the earth, after being here for thousands and thousands of years. The idea of saving a species, even a subspecies, may seem arrogant. But who else was going to do it?"

"Wolves represent something," Lori says. "They are social like humans, but they are also wild. *Wild.* I just spent five days in jail for protesting a ski resort in Colorado. I thought about wolves—and about jaguars—the whole time. We used to have wild jaguars in Arizona and New Mexico. I felt just like a trapped wolf or jaguar in its zoo or breeding pen. I've been arrested. We've all been arrested."

"There are lots of reasons why," Carol speaks briskly. "Wolves are mystical. I've heard that one, and I agree. But it's not something I say to ranchers. For some people, you know, wolf reintroduction is just an ego trip, something to shove down the throat of the livestock industry. For me, I like the idea of an entire ecosystem. Predators like wolves belong in the Southwest."

"If we can be successful with the Mexican wolf," Sue Larson says, "with a species that we strove so hard to eradicate, then maybe we have a chance with other species. Maybe, too, we have a responsibility to make amends, to the species themselves, to *ourselves.* Maybe, ultimately, reintroducing the wolf is a selfish thing. Wolves are missing. It's a sadness to have them gone. We took a land of teeming wildlife and brought many animals to the point of extinction. *We have to do everything we can to reverse that trend.*"

"Lines are being drawn," Dan Moore agrees. "We can try and re-inhabit the North American continent, repopulate some of its wild-life, change the way people travel and make their economy. Or we can have the total commoditization of everything. The dream or the nightmare."

As Lori says, wolves represent something.

This must come from the heart.

The Southwest would be a better place if thirty-two wolves lived at the White Sands Missile Range, killing deer and bearing pups in the pinon-juniper, oak and ponderosa pine forests of the San Andres and Oscuras mountains. The Southwest would be better still if forty more wolves hunted southeastern Arizona in the Galiuro and Pi-nalenos, the Chiricahuas, and Atascosa mountains. The state of Texas would be improved if a pack of radio-collared *lobos* patterned Big Bend National Park with their scent markings and territorial signs. All Americans would feel better if we could agree to share our public land with one hundred Mexican wolves, a fraction of the wildness that once was here.

Either you think so or you don't.

Lines are being drawn; we are remapping once again the world of the wolf.

In North Carolina, fifteen red wolves were released into the Alligator National Wildlife Refuge in 1987. The captive-raised animals produced four litters; more red wolves were set free on islands off the southeastern seaboard; still more are planned for the Great Smoky Mountains National Park. In North Carolina, wolves have become part of the tourist industry. One town even has adopted the red wolf as its symbol. It helped that this animal is relatively small and does not usually eat cattle or sheep. It also helped that the Fish and Wildlife Service put a lot of time and energy into public education. "Wolves don't wait at school-bus stops, don't dig up graves, don't lurk waiting to attack," assured the biologists, again and again, to group after group. The recovery of the red wolf is considered something of a miracle—and a model for the Mexican wolf program.

In Minnesota, people also have grown to appreciate their more than 1,500 wolves. Minnesota wolves often are held up as an example of how "good" wolves can be. Here, some 7,200 farms and ranches are interspersed throughout the wolf's range. But from 1976 through 1990, only nine to fifty-five farms annually reported verified wolf depredations. The highest cattle loss claimed by ranchers was in 1990, about 4.7 cows per 10,000 available victims. The highest sheep loss claimed was in 1981, 26.6 sheep lost per 10,000 sheep. A state program compensates farmers and ranchers for these losses. In 1989, the Minnesota Department of Agriculture paid out $43,663 to forty farmers (seventy-seven claims were made and seventy-six paid) for 1 bull, 6 cows, 3 yearlings, 52 calves, 13 ewes, 32 lambs, and 1,866 turkeys.

Clearly, wolves are not invisible. They seem, for example, to really like turkeys, and they occasionally kill dogs. In 1990, ninety-five gray wolves—accused of "interfacing" badly with people and their food—were trapped and shot by the Animal Damage Control program.

In the West, significantly, wolves from Canada have migrated into Glacier National Park and are moving south. In western Montana, there may be forty to fifty wolves; another ten or twenty may live in Idaho. These remain a federally designated endangered species. Illegally killing a wolf in the lower forty-eight states can mean a big fine. In Montana, Defenders of Wildlife also has set up a $100,000 compensation program for ranchers.

The best-known and longest wolf controversy is centered in Wyoming's Yellowstone National Park. By the 1930s, the National Park Service had eliminated the wolf in this area. Fifty years later, the same Park Service solemnly approved the Northern Rocky Mountain Wolf Recovery Plan. A 1987 revised plan proposed the release of an experimental group; as with the Mexican wolves in White Sands, the label "experimental" means that "problem" animals can legally be killed or removed. Under the 1987 plan, when the population has grown to include ten breeding pairs in ten packs of seven to ten animals, and when these ten pairs have lived in Yellowstone for three consecutive years, then the wolf can be delisted from its endangered status.

Yellowstone—says nearly every biologist in the country—is a perfect place for reintroduction. It is begging for wolves. The Yellowstone recovery area is the largest intact ecosystem in the temperate zone of the earth: 8.5 million acres of national park, national forest, and undeveloped wildland. Intact, at least, but for the wolf. An eventual population of 50 to 150 wolves here could reduce elk by 15 to 20 percent, bison by 10 percent, mule deer by 20 percent, and moose by 10 percent. This in itself would be a very good thing, since it has become clear that elk, in particular, are overgrazing the national park. Wolves are not expected to affect ranchers much. The prey base is too great and there are relatively few ranches in the area—far fewer, say, than in Minnesota. Wolves would not affect a simultaneous plan to recover the grizzly bear. Wolves are not a threat to park visitors; healthy wild wolves rarely attack humans. Nor would wolves significantly hinder public use of the park. Few people, in fact, would ever see these shy animals, although we might be lucky enough to hear them howl.

This one should have been easy.

In the late 1980s, however, a number of bills put before Congress to start wolf reintroduction in Yellowstone were defeated. Western politicians had gone slightly crazy. A Montana representative compared wolves to cockroaches; a senator from that state predicted that once wolves were in Yellowstone "there'll be a dead child within a year." Public meetings were emotional. Ranchers were concerned with wolves eating their cows and sheep. Some rural residents feared for their lives. Hunters worried about the wolf's impact on wildlife. Many saw wolf reintroduction as just another way of "locking people out" of the public lands.

In the end, a federally mandated Wolf Management Committee recommended that *all* existing and reintroduced wolves (with the exception of those in Glacier National Park and the surrounding area) be considered a nonessential, experimental population. This meant that naturally recolonizing wolves in Montana and Idaho could also legally be killed by ranchers on public and private land. (To kill such a wolf now, of course, is to kill an endangered species and to commit a federal crime.) In essence, the committee tried to bypass the Endangered Species Act and reclassify the endangered status of wolves.

Out of the ten-member committee, two were from environmental organizations. They voted against the proposal, complaining that it was not a "roadmap to wolf recovery, but a roadblock." Defenders of Wildlife took their cue from Dan Moore and Lori Fish. They threatened to sue the secretary of the interior, the director of the U.S. Fish and Wildlife Service, and the director of national parks for refusing to comply with the endangered species law.

Congress was not pleased. Instead of accepting the committee's plan, they ordered an environmental impact statement, the first major step toward recovery. If all goes well, wolves could be reintroduced into the national park as an experimental, nonessential population as early as 1994.

Some people are laying bets that wolves from Montana and Idaho will get there first, on their own.

Some people believe that they already *are* there, and that reintroduction is a big mistake; naturally occurring wolves have the protection of the Endangered Species Act, whereas reintroduced wolves can be killed and manipulated for too many reasons.

This is what Pamela Brown believes. "The purpose of my work," she says, "is to allow wolves to reestablish naturally."

Pam has heard stories of wild Mexican wolves being seen—and shot—in the Southwest. She thinks that a viable population still exists in Mexico. She opposes compensation programs as payoffs that encourage careless husbandry. She looks at all the money being spent on reintroduction and believes that it could be better spent—on the training of herders and guard dogs, on public education, on programs for children.

Environmentalists do agree on one thing: wolves would have been in Yellowstone long ago, and in the Southwest as well, were it not for ranchers and the political clout of ranchers.

Some of this is changing. In a few states, such as Arizona, the Cattleman's Association has announced that its members can live with wolf reintroduction as long as they can control "problem animals." Ranchers who follow Allan Savory are more radical: they actively want the predators back to rile up cows and generate hoof action. There are even a few ranchers who simply like the idea of wild wolves and who think, secretly, that wolves are mystical.

Still, by and large, most cowboys remain hostile.

"They sit around their kitchen table, and they talk about wolves and all the damage that wolves do," Carol Martingdale says. "But the wolf was gone fifty years ago! These are tales that their granddad is telling, things that he saw or heard about from his own father. Ranchers today have no experience with wolves. It's folklore and mythology. The stories get bigger and bigger."

"They've demonized the wolf!" Dan Moore agrees. "Wolves are

the criminals of the animal world that we evil environmentalists are trying to release from prison."

Recently, in a rare chain of events, I was invited to a local Cow-belle meeting—an organization of women interested in promoting the livestock industry. Teenagers stood up before this crowd and talked about trips sponsored by the Cowbelles, about how to cook hamburgers, about how to raise leaner cows. Later, I wandered over to a table in the corner of the room and picked up a pamphlet. I don't know who brought it. I don't know who believed it. It showed graphic pictures of wolves eating bighorn sheep in Alaska.

"Wildlife is in trouble today," wrote the author of this tract titled "What Everyone Who Enjoys Wildlife Should Know." "It's not a loss of habitat. . . . Hunting is not the problem either. . . . The problem is PREDATION." The pamphlet noted that "predation is nonspecific— meaning the predator takes what it finds" and that "predators are the main carriers of deadly diseases of wildlife."

This latter comment seemed as odd as the first. I read on.

Further down came the breaking news that "most environmental groups are anti-God, anti-American and anti-gun (in the hands of law-abiding citizens)." I was urged to "Join ABUNDANT WILDLIFE SOCIETY today." I could have, too, for $25.

By the year 2000, there will—I hope—be wolves in small pockets across the West. All that we know of wolves, and all that we don't, will be going on in the remote mountains of Montana, Idaho, Wyoming, Arizona, and New Mexico. We spent the first half of the twentieth century poisoning and shooting this species to extinction. We'll spend the latter part trying to bring the wolf back. No one can accuse us of being consistent. But perhaps you can say we are maturing.

"To regret deeply," said Thoreau, "is to live afresh."

"*The most important issue I see in terms of wolf conservation is basically wilderness preservation. I believe there's not enough wilderness left in the world right now, and we're never going to get any more. Our wilderness will continue to diminish, and that's why one of the best contributions to wolf conservation is to try and hold the line on preserving wilderness, whether it's in the United States or Canada or wherever.*"
—L. David Mech

"*When I entered this sublime wilderness the day was nearly done, the trees with rosy, glowing countenances seemed to be hushed and thoughtful, as if waiting in conscious religious dependence on the sun, and one naturally walked softly and awe-stricken among them. I wandered on, meeting nobler trees where all was noble, subdued in the general calm, as if in some vast hall pervaded by the deepest sanctities and solemnities that sway human souls. At sundown the trees seemed to cease their worship and breathe free.*"
—John Muir

We tell stories. We tell stories to ourselves and to our children, and this is how we know the world. These stories are the basis of our daily decisions: what kind of clothes we wear and when we wear them, what we eat, who we marry, where we live, the purpose of our lives, the purpose of our dying. In the range war between cowboys and environmentalists, stories and myths are clearly as important as facts. In our differing "physics of beauty," Animal Damage Control represents hope to one side and destruction to the other. The re-introduction of the wolf is a return to wildness at its worst or at its best. Related to both—perhaps the most complex, encompass-ing, and emotional issue of all—is wilderness and wilderness preservation.

Once again, the lines are clearly drawn.

Most environmentalists are passionately for the protection of wil-derness areas and the legislation of new ones. They see around the very word *wilderness* a numinous halo. For them, wilderness is not merely a valuable resource in a competitive free-market system. Wilderness is sacred space.

Most ranchers accept our current wilderness areas with grudging resignation. They are puzzled by the insistence that we need more. They see eviction in the word *wilderness*; they see government, tyranny, and fraud.

From a national perspective, we are a culture born in the wild. When the first Europeans came to this continent, the "wilderness," of course, was already home to millions of Native Americans. For the English and Spanish and French, wilderness (and its inhabitants) be-came the enemy to conquer. That job was barely done before we be-gan to mourn our loss. Just as the cowboy is a peculiarly American character, the frontier—the entry into wilderness—is a peculiarly American place.

Significantly, a history of wilderness is best expressed as a history of legislation. In 1872, President Ulysses S. Grant took two million acres of Wyoming and called it Yellowstone National Park. From that point on, the government increasingly set aside land in an effort to protect its natural resources, if not necessarily its wilderness values. By the late nineteenth century, men like John Muir could legiti-mately be called modern champions of wilderness preservation—an idea that included aesthetic, cultural, scientific, and spiritual concerns.

With the advent of the car and an expanding system of roads, the need to designate some areas as "undeveloped" became more clear. In 1924 the Gila Primitive Area in southwestern New Mexico was the first formally protected wilderness in the United States and probably in the world. The Forest Service continued to establish primitive or wild areas, from which they prohibited roads (except for access to private property), logging, and motorized vehicles. Grazing was allowed, as were motorboats and airplanes.

It was the usual tug-of-war, between conservationists and commodity interests. Finally, in 1964, the Wilderness Act passed by Congress defined a National Wilderness Preservation System of 9.1 million acres. The act directed federal agencies to search for, study, and report on new potential wilderness sites. Mining was to continue in wilderness areas until January 1, 1984; after that, no further claims could be made. The grazing of livestock, where established before the date of the act, was permitted indefinitely.

The Wilderness Act has probably been quoted more than any other piece of recent legislation. Its beginning is particularly majestic.

In order to assure that an increasing population, accompanied by expanding settlement and growing mechanization, does not occupy and modify all areas within the United States and its possessions, leaving no lands designated for preservation and protection in their natural condition, it is hereby declared to be the policy of the Congress to secure for the American people of present and future generations the benefits of an enduring resource of wilderness.

The act further defines its terms. "A wilderness, in contrast with those areas where man and his own works dominate the landscape, is hereby recognized as an area where the earth and its community of life are untrammeled by man." Wilderness also should provide "outstanding opportunities for solitude or a primitive and unconfined type of recreation" "with the imprint of man's work substantially unnoticeable."

Given such language, the inclusion of grazing was an obvious contradiction—and a necessary compromise. Without this compromise, there would have been no Wilderness Act.

This is as true today as it was thirty years ago.

In 1980, two House Committee reports emphasized the rights of livestock growers. These directives were aimed specifically and sternly at the Forest Service. "There shall be no curtailments of grazing in wilderness areas simply because an area is, or has been, designated as wilderness, nor should wilderness designations be used as an excuse by administrators to slowly 'phase out' grazing," the report chastised. "It is anticipated that the numbers of livestock permitted to graze in wilderness would remain at the approximate levels existing at the time an area enters the wilderness system."

That system has grown from 9.1 million acres to over 94 million. The Forest Service has almost 18 percent of its land in wilderness; the National Park Service has 49 percent; the Fish and Wildlife Service has 23 percent; and the Bureau of Land Management has less than 1 percent. (This last figure should change as western states submit new wilderness bills that include BLM land.) Almost two-thirds of wilderness is in Alaska. About 4.5 percent is east of the Mississippi River, with nearly half of that in Florida's Everglades National Park. Overall, in the lower forty-eight states, less than 2 percent of land is designated as wilderness. Roughly half of wildernesses in the West are grazed.

"I believe we have enough," a rancher in my valley tells me. He runs cows on a wilderness allotment and he wearies of the restrictions involved: he cannot drive his truck to his stock tanks; he cannot build new stock tanks easily or without permission; he cannot use a chain saw to cut down fence posts. He sees the wilderness as a place where he lives and works, and he does not like the sense of being shut out. He does not like the idea that he is a visitor, not a citizen. His voice rises in frustration. "I don't see why people think we need any more!"

"Our goal is to double the size of the National Wilderness Preservation System in the next twenty-five years," a woman from the Wilderness Society says. We sit in her office, with its big glass panels overlooking Denver's skyline. "I love my job," she speaks with fervor. "I couldn't ask for a better thing to be doing with my life."

My husband and I met in graduate school in Missoula, Montana. We were in our mid-twenties, propelled biologically and culturally to "settle down," find a home, and take root. I wanted to return to the Southwest, and so we spent many nights poring over maps of Arizona and New Mexico. We picked Silver City because of how it looked on these maps. Its population is small, about twelve thousand, and it is fifty miles from an interstate highway, which meant, we hoped, that it would not experience the growth I had seen in Phoenix and Tucson. The town is also close to the Gila National Forest and boasts a modest university. Most important, Silver City is "The Gateway to the Gila Wilderness," the nation's first and the Southwest's largest. This is rugged and remote country. This is more than five hundred thousand acres of wilderness wrapped in a numinous halo—wild, harsh, fertile, and mysterious.

In the first four months of 1981, we married, moved to Silver City, got jobs, and bought land in the nearby Mimbres Valley. When we climbed the ridge behind our twelve acres, we could see the edge of the national forest. Farther north, beyond sight, was the invisible border that separates wilderness from a more mundane world. We counted the miles from where we stood: fourteen as the crow flies. We wanted to be nearer. At the same time, we thought ourselves lucky, to be as near as we were.

There are many reasons for preserving wilderness areas. The environmental philosopher Holmes Rolston III has cataloged these for us: life support value (pollution scrubbing, hydrologic cycles, wildlife habitat, insect regulation); scientific value ("destroying wildlands is like burning unread books"); genetic diversity value (useful products such as medicines and crops yet undiscovered); aesthetic value ("experiences unlikely to be had in the Metropolitan Museum"); cultural symbolization value (the bald eagle as more than another species of bird); historical value ("the profoundest historical museum of all"); character-building value ("a place to sweat, to push yourself more than usual"); therapeutic value (a number of programs take mentally disturbed persons into the wilderness); religious value (a natural temple); and intrinsic value (wilderness has a right, in and of itself, to exist).

I would add one more.

A newly hatched chick, dazed and still wet, will run when the shadow of a hawk passes overhead. The chick will not run when this shadow is that of a pigeon or heron. Chickens are born knowing the very shape and image of fear; in the same way, humans also are born with inherent psychic structures. Even the basic principles of grammar may well be innate and not learned. The psychologist Carl Jung wrote that certain ideas and images, certain stories, are "a memory deposit, an engram, derived from the condensation of innumerable similar experiences." Wilderness is an experience that humans have known for most of their evolutionary development. Thoreau said that "in wildness is the preservation of the world." It may also be the preservation of humanity. We have an ancient psychic root sunk deep into wilderness. It is our source and primal imprint. This is part of the intensity that surrounds this word for so many people. This is why my husband and I thought ourselves lucky.

In the end, we did not immerse ourselves in wilderness adventures and backpacking trips. We immersed ourselves, as our species does, in being social and gregarious: in teaching, writing, building a house, making friends, and making babies. In our first year, we probably went into the wilderness three or four times. That number dropped to once, maybe twice, when we had small children.

Ranchers who oppose wilderness areas might find this significant.

They are wrong. Wilderness is an idea, like love or God, that may be experienced rarely but that remains crucial to our sense of meaning. Wilderness is an anchor that must exist in the outside world to be fully held in the mind. I cannot easily imagine an earth that has no or too little wilderness. That thought is truly appalling—and truly disorienting.

"How little is too little?" my rancher friend asks.

I suddenly feel greedy. I operate out of fear and a great sense of imbalance. The weight of every shopping mall overwhelms me. How many acres of wilderness to counteract Disneyland? How many can restore optimism in a world where the majority of rivers are polluted, where the forests are disappearing, where the very sky is falling down?

More, I say in my heart. More, more, more! I want all the wilderness I can get. Double the size of the national system? Let's triple it! Let 6 percent of the contiguous United States be wilderness. Ten percent! Fifteen! While we're at it, let's make it a *real* wilderness. Let's kick those cows and sheep off. Let's allow the streams to fill with sedge and watercress and willow and cottonwood and sycamore and alder. Let's bring the water back. Let's give the grass and meadows and trees to wildlife. Let's give them to the wolf and grizzly bear.

I want the dream. I want more.

I feel, at times, something of the anger that Steve Johnson feels. Early explorers of the Mimbres Valley and nearby Gila River often spoke of hearing wolves and, on occasion, of seeing them frisk about at play. Today, everyone knows that the Gila Wilderness would be a great place to reintroduce the Mexican wolf. "Of course, no one says that out loud," Dan Moore confesses. "Wolves will never be in the Gila again because of the ranching community there. We all whisper to ourselves, *the Gila, the Gila.* But it's impossible."

Dan Moore is right. Of the 3.3 million acres in the Gila National Forest, 2.8 million are part of someone's ranch. Some 31 percent of the Gila Wilderness is grazed; nearly 100 percent of the adjacent

Aldo Leopold Wilderness is grazed; more than 87 percent of the nearby Blue Range Wilderness is grazed. The ranchers who have cows here are the most conservative in New Mexico and among the most conservative in America. Indeed, next-door Catron County actually passed a local (although probably illegal) ordinance that prohibits Federal Service rangers from reducing AUMs on public-lands grazing allotments. Theoretically, the federal employees could be arrested and taken to county jail for doing their job. These ranchers are vehement that their "right" to graze is being abused. Because of their strong opposition, there will never be wolves again in the Gila. These men will continue, righteously, to kill mountain lion and black bear. If they can, they will prevent the designation of new wilderness areas in nearby BLM land. We will not take the opportunity, here, to pass on something that is wilder than the way we found it.

The thought grieves me more than seems reasonable. My generation has lost the belief that our children's lives will be better than our own. We know that our sons and daughters will inherit an earth made shabbier and less abundant. *We must do everything we can to reverse that trend.* I walk through a Gila Wilderness that has been largely tamed. Yet my daughter—this is the story I tell myself—could walk the same land made rich with the presence of its original predators. Her senses would be more alert. Her consciousness would be heightened. In this small instance, in this one place, it could be better for her than it was for me.

The door slams shut. Something that I want is on the other side. Ranchers have what I want, and I feel angry. I feel afraid for the future of my children. I have inchoate fears and inchoate anger and inchoate guilt.

These emotions lash at the environmentalist, and they lash at the rancher. These emotions drive us. They whip us across the desert floor where we run, headlong, without thought.

We have to be careful now.

It is necessary to look at our process of storytelling.

In truth, there is no wilderness "untrammeled by man," and there hasn't been for a very long time. Human beings have been altering the earth for millions of years: hunting, gathering, planting, pruning, sowing, managing, and mismanaging. In North America, Paleo-Indians contributed to the extinction of a number of big game species. By 1491, there were possibly one hundred million people living in this hemisphere. Rather soon, Europeans also were swarming over the landscape, poking into every corner and swamp. When John Muir walked through the Sierra Mountains, he saw a wilderness that needed to be preserved. He did not see how purposefully the Miwok Indians of this region had already changed the vegetation: setting fires under oaks to remove duff infested with acorn weevil and pruning big-leaf maples to produce the straight sprouts needed for basketry. Like the cow, we are a powerful species, altering every ecosystem we enter. We come from nature, we are nature, we change nature, and we consume nature.

What wilderness we do know is an administrative concept. It is a law and a misnomer. Much of the emotion in wilderness issues comes from the fact that in 1964 Congress did not use more realistic language. Cows would make sense in a primitive ranch area or an undeveloped wildland. They seem absurd in a wilderness! Yet, in every case where grazing is now allowed, that wilderness *was* being grazed by cows the day before its legal transformation—and it was grazed by cows the day after. The process continues with the legislation of new "wildernesses." From a rancher's point of view, this is simple sleight of hand.

The irony of wilderness is that it must be more regulated than any other public land. On wilderness rivers, recreationists pack out their own human wastes. In the wilderness ethic, going off established trails is frowned on. Gas stoves are preferable to campfires. Wildflow-

ers should not be picked. Pets are better left at home. It is not easy
for us to tread lightly. It is not even natural.

The Gila Wilderness is a good story.

For thousands of years, these mountains and forests were popu-
lated by hunters and gatherers and farmers. Their homes are everywhere. Pick a place where you would like to live, and it is likely that
someone else lived there before you. Cliff houses blended into the
caves. Villages grew up by the rivers. An extensive art industry
thrived; pottery produced during the classical period of the Mim-
breno Indians is world famous today and can be found discreetly ad-
vertised in the back pages of *The New Yorker.* Then, around A.D. 1300,
these Mogollon people mysteriously "disappeared," probably because of drought and an overuse of natural resources. The Apache
came next, sometime before 1500, and stayed until they were driven
away by the Spanish, the Mexicans, and the Americans. The late
nineteenth century saw the usual wholesale overgrazing. In 1899,
President McKinley formed the Gila River Forest Reserve, and in
1907 this was placed under the newly created Forest Service. Cattle
and sheep continued to dominate the area's ecology.

In 1909, a recent graduate from the Yale Forest School began
working for the Forest Service in the Southwest. Aldo Leopold was
an avid sportsman. His initial plan for the Gila Wilderness, which he
helped establish in 1924, was that it provide a national hunting
ground and paradise for outdoor recreationists. Leopold married into
an old southwestern ranching family; as a game manager, he vowed
to exterminate every calf-eating predator in New Mexico "down to
the last wolf and lion." As we all know, Aldo Leopold's vision ma-
tured. Above all, he came to regret his role in killing off natural
predators.

"I have watched the face of many a newly wolfless mountain," he
wrote, "and seen the south-facing slopes wrinkle with a maze of

new deer trails. I have seen every edible bush and seedling browsed, first to anemic desuetude, and then to death. I have seen every edible tree defoliated to the height of a saddlehorn. . . . I now suspect that just as a deer herd lives in mortal fear of its wolves, so does a mountain live in mortal fear of its deer."

He might have been writing directly about the Gila. In the early 1930s, a bloated deer population in the wilderness prompted the North Star Road to be built to provide access to hunters. The road cut the Gila Wilderness in half; the section east of the new road was renamed the Black Range Primitive Area. Wilderness, it seemed, could easily be repackaged. In 1955, more land was sliced away to allow for the mining of fluorite. In 1957 yet another road was punched through for tourists on their way to the Gila Cliff Dwellings National Monument. The area to the east of this road was redesignated the Gila Primitive Area. Then, in 1980, these acres were reclassified once more, back to Gila Wilderness, with the Black Range Primitive Area rerenamed the Aldo Leopold Wilderness.

It was all a bit confusing to old-time ranchers.

They put their heads down and kept on cowboying.

In 1990, 9,438 cows and yearlings grazed in the Gila and Aldo Leopold wildernesses. Eight of the twenty-eight wilderness grazing allotments were determined by the Forest Service to be overstocked or declining in condition. Seventeen were not being managed to meet the Forest Service's objectives.

The largest grazing area in these wildernesses is the Diamond Bar allotment, more than 145,000 acres of which about 85,000 are considered grazeable rangeland. The grazing permit for this ranch was issued in 1908. In 1924, the year that the Gila became a wilderness, the Diamond Bar Cattle Company was running 2,300 cows. The ranch would change hands seven more times, with increasing reductions in its stock numbers, until by 1980—when the allotment was rereclassified as the Gila and Aldo Leopold wildernesses—the permitted numbers had dropped to 1,188 cows year-round.

In 1982 and 1983, the Forest Service evaluated the range and suggested that this number should fall to 833 cows. The 1983 Forest Service Environmental Assessment Report pointed to a range that was, ominously, 76 percent in poor condition and 23 percent in fair condition.

In 1984, the permittee on the Diamond Bar allotment went bankrupt. The ranch, with its associated permit, was taken into receivership by the First Intermediate Credit Bank of Texas. As the bank tried to sell its new property, the Forest Service announced its decision to reduce the cows on the allotment. The bank responded quickly, claiming that the reduction would cost them $500,000 in property value. The New Mexico State University Range Improvement Task Force—an arm of the state's cattlegrower's association—was brought in to examine the Forest Service's data.

At this point, there are two versions.

The Forest Service says that when it, too, reexamined its information, a number of mathematical errors were found. This is why the Forest Service renegotiated a new management plan with the First Intermediate Credit Bank of Texas, one that allowed the original 1,188 cattle, with a temporary nonuse of 188 head while improvements such as fifteen new water tanks were being constructed.

Some environmentalists, however, believe that the Forest Service was simply intimidated by the bank and by the Range Improvement Task Force. In Don Oman's words, government officials were motivated by fear—"the fear of political pressure, the fear of offending the livestock industry, the fear of risking our jobs."

In 1985, the bank sold the Diamond Bar to a family partnership. These were fourth generation New Mexican ranchers who bought the ranch, admittedly, because "it was cheap." The Diamond Bar was cheap because it depended on a wilderness allotment of harsh terrain and declining waters that no one else wanted. In any case, a ninety-five-acre base property, a ranch house with outbuildings, and an attached grazing permit to run more than one thousand cows on federal land still involved a considerable amount of money.

A letter from the Forest Service warned these buyers, officially, that the attached grazing permit was *not* real property.

"Although we have made no formal appraisal," wrote the forest supervisor, "the loan amount greatly exceeds the fair market value of the listed collateral. This is no problem for the United States as long as you and your lender realize that this instrument implies that there is absolutely no value assigned to the Term Grazing Permit itself. Any loan amount in excess of the fair market value of the collateral alone is at the personal risk of the lender and is to be considered unsecured."

By most accounts, the ranchers on the Diamond Bar are serious, conscientious, hardworking, likable people—two sisters, their mother, and two sons-in-law. Like many other ranchers, they believe that their grazing lease is a right, not a privilege. They argue that there *is* value assigned to the permit, and that they "purchased improvements" on the federal land when they "bought that permit." They believe there is enough wilderness that is not being grazed. Moreover, they believe that ungrazed streams fill up with trees, which soak up water and lower the water table. They believe that those parts of the Gila Wilderness that have no cows are overgrown with vegetation. They can quote from Allan Savory.

At the same time, these ranchers understood, rather soon, that not even fifteen new water tanks would be enough to keep their cattle from overusing the allotment's three major riparian areas: South Diamond Creek, home to the threatened and endangered Gila trout; Black Canyon, a popular hiking area; and the East Fork of the Gila River, another popular site that also contained three threatened and endangered fish species. If the "resource was to be protected," there had to be more water in the uplands made available to cows. In 1987, the permittees asked the Forest Service to allow them to use bulldozers to put in forty-five additional stock tanks. (A stock or water tank is usually a pond gouged out of the ground by mechanical equipment. Such tanks, replenished only by rainwater, often turn into brown, muddy, smelly mires from which cow trails radiate.) Accordingly, an integrated resource management team was set up to determine a new management plan.

Nearly five years later, when a draft of that plan was released to the public, the Diamond Bar allotment became another symbol.

The IRM team had come up with six alternatives. Alternative A was a "No Action," which meant simply that existing developments would be maintained. Alternatives B, C, and D reduced cow numbers respectively to 300, 600, and 800, with varying degrees of new developments. Alternative E was proposed by the permittees. It included the forty-five new stock tanks, forty miles of fence, and two miles of trail. The ranchers would pay $167,000 for these improvements, and the government would pay $56,000. The permitted numbers would remain at 1,188, with the allotment divided into ten pastures.

Alternative F was the Forest Service's preferred choice. It also kept the numbers at 1,188 cows. It included thirty-seven new stock tanks and twenty-eight miles of fence, with a rotation system that used the Black Canyon and South Diamond Creek riparian areas for a period of sixty days for two years out of three. By resting these areas during the main growing season, the Forest Service hoped to encourage new stands of willow and cottonwood. This plan would cost the permittees $123,000. The government's share was $41,000.

An important change in the 1992 draft plan was a reanalysis of the range. The current range conservationist had gone over the 1979 field data once again. He discovered that the 1984 Forest Service report had been inaccurate in this assessment as well: in fact, three-fourths of the allotment was in fair condition, not poor. The riparian areas, admittedly, were in terrible shape. But the overall range trend from 1965 to 1978 was upward.

Environmentalists, to say the least, were skeptical.

In a series of public meetings and forums and newsletters, they challenged the Forest Service's judgment. Much of the protest was local. "The Forest Service," said one spokeswoman from the newly formed group Gila Watch, "is proposing to turn the wilderness into a giant stockyard, using bulldozers to fell trees and scrape out water tanks."

National organizations also were alarmed. Bulldozers in the wilderness! Thirty-seven new stock tanks! This kind of precedent could threaten the integrity of other wilderness areas. Even moderates were concerned that the Forest Service had not gone out into the field to update their information. The 1979 range data was fourteen years old. The analysis of it was controversial.

Some people felt that the Forest Service had been deceptive. Not only were the mathematical errors too convenient, but the alternatives listed by the IRM team seemed inadequate. Only the Forest Service's preferred choice, alternative F, made any real attempt to protect the stream areas. And was it really a feasible plan? If a thousand cattle were allowed into South Diamond and Black Canyon for sixty days during the early spring, wouldn't they effectively eliminate all the young tree shoots?

As important, if water was developed in the uplands, wouldn't that disrupt the ecological balance of those areas? Were the uplands to be the next sacrifice?

And why, on the Diamond Bar allotment (as in the rest of the national forest), was the Forest Service allocating 75 percent of available forage for livestock *and only 25 percent for wildlife?*

What did alternative F mean for the endangered Gila trout and for other endangered fish species?

What, after all, was the point of wilderness?

Forest Service officials listened. They nodded, they sighed, they commiserated. They opened up their books and freely showed the mathematical errors. They admitted to losing some key reports. They also agreed to update their field data and reevaluate range conditions. Then they pointed to the congressional guidelines given to them in 1980: "There shall be no curtailment of grazing permits or privileges in an area simply because it is designated as wilderness" and "The construction of new improvements or replacement of deteriorating facilities in wilderness is permissible if in accordance with those guidelines and management plans governing the area involved."

Environmentalists were also poring over these guidelines. Their attention focused on another passage: "However, the construction of new improvements should be primarily for the purpose of resource protection and the more effective management of these resources rather than to accommodate increased numbers of livestock."

The key phrase was "resource protection." Did the House Committee mean the resource of wilderness? Or the resource of the range?

The Forest Service was not trying to increase livestock numbers. But it *was* trying hard to maintain the numbers already there. As the district ranger reasoned, "If this wasn't a wilderness, we'd definitely put in those stock tanks in order to protect the riparian areas. So if we don't put in the stock tanks to protect wilderness values and then reduce cows to protect those streams, aren't we reducing cows because it is a wilderness? That is specifically what we have been told *not* to do."

The Forest Service believed that the ranchers on the Diamond Bar were people with whom the government could work. If these permittees went bankrupt, the next ones might not be so reasonable. Management, not numbers, was the key. The cows could be reduced, even drastically reduced, and still do a lot of damage if they were not controlled.

Most important, the range specialists in the district thought that alternative F *was* feasible and *would* help recover the stream areas. At any rate, they meant to do a lot of monitoring. They would change the plan if necessary.

A few environmentalists even worried that a decision against ranchers on the Diamond Bar could limit new wilderness areas on BLM land. If ranchers thought that a wilderness designation meant a reduction in cows, if agreements about grazing were not being honored, then the entire livestock industry would oppose wilderness even more strongly. The choice might be between land that was grazed, scarred by stock tanks, but still roadless—and land that was grazed, scarred by stock tanks, and cut by roads as well.

The heart of wilderness was a tangle of politics.

The Forest Service threw up its hands.

"Environmental groups may sue us if we don't reduce cow numbers on this allotment," said one official. "But other groups—the permittees and people who are trying to protect the ranchers' interests—will sue us if we do."

"I guess," said the man, half-relieved, "we may have to let the courts decide this one."

By January 1993, the Forest Service did not yet have a new management plan for the Diamond Bar ranch. Instead, they had developed yet another preferred alternative. This one also, stubbornly, kept cow numbers at 1,188. But it required only twenty-three stock tanks, with half the herd in yearlings (who distribute better and can be kept further from water). Suddenly the Black Canyon and South Diamond riparian areas were not being grazed at all, although a "10 to 15 percent utilization of the bottoms" by intransigent cows "would not be considered inappropriate." This plan also had to be reviewed by the U.S. Fish and Wildlife Service to determine if it endangered the recovery of native fish.

It was a conciliatory gesture.

Most opponents were not conciliated. The Forest Service could refine its management plan until doomsday. The fact remained that many environmentalists did not want *any* new developments—or bulldozers—in the wilderness. They did not believe that over a thousand cows should be on the Diamond Bar allotment. Like Denzel Ferguson, some did not think that any cows should be there at all.

To paraphrase Lori Fish, "We've already lost wilderness if we can't protect it. What good is a wilderness designation if it can't be enforced?"

From our small adobe house, my husband and I drive a dirt road, across the rising Mimbres River, onto a two-lane state highway. After fifteen miles, we turn east up another dirt road, the very one that in 1930 cut the Gila Wilderness in half. From here, it takes over an hour of twisting, turning, and bumping to reach the trailhead that leads into Black Canyon. My children are five and eight now. More frequently, we take them on day hikes into the Gila Wilderness, walks that often are shorter than we had planned and longer than they tolerate without complaining.

The first mile of this trip is defined by cows. Their excrement, old and new, litters the trail, with clouds of flies and gnats buzzing up from the new. For now, Black Canyon is grazed every other year, and this is the year. It is spring, a phenomenal spring of more rain that anyone has ever seen before. We scare off group after group of mother cows with calves, and we eye them as warily as they eye us. A few shake their heads in menace and maternal warning. My five-year-old son is fascinated. In the last year, his desire to be a cowboy has only intensified; he is saving up his birthday money to buy a ranch. I cannot explain his obsession, no more than I can dismiss it.

"How much does a cow cost?" he asks, as he has many times before. "Are these wild cows? How many cows should I have on *my* ranch? Why is that cow looking at us? Why can't bulls have babies? Is that a bull? Why do cows have horns? Why can't I get closer?"

We walk by a small inholding of private property. Across a pasture fenced off for horses, over the stream that feeds this canyon, we see the metal roof of the house where the permittees on the Diamond Bar allotment live. Only one couple stays out here now and manages the ranch. I have been to meetings with this man and woman. I have eaten lunch with them and laughed at their jokes. I have watched them grow angry as environmentalists accused them of damaging the public land. These are people who never thought they would be standing up in a crowd to defend their livelihood. They are caught in the middle of something they had not anticipated. They bought a ranch. They signed a permit agreement. Everyone important in our society was there: the government, the bank, the lawyers.

We pass by a messy area littered with downed trees, branches, and wood chips. Beavers have been at work. My daughter explains this to me, and I am impressed. Did I know so much about beavers at her age? We pass through a blowdown, where the big dead cotton-woods are fallen soldiers, angled against each other, bleached gray. Although the grasses here have already been grazed once this season, they are rising again, rich and green. The dainty heads of blue grama knock at our ankles and knees. The stream is fifteen feet wide and tumbles past noisily. We hear the whistle, trill, and caw of blue jays and brown towhees. We start to enter the most beautiful country in the world.

Graciously, my husband allows me to run on ahead. He knows how much I enjoy this. I love to run on trails. I love to run through the forest, jumping over logs, navigating water, brought up suddenly, then bounding downhill. The thick vertical lines of ponderosa pine blur. Yellow and white wildflowers flicker in the grass. Such patterns are a jumble in the uncertainty of my peripheral vision; the ground is what I must concentrate on. Rocks, incline, sticks, holes. I match myself to these.

All my running—and I have been a runner, off and on, for twenty years—is based on this kind of fantasy. I am a deer. I am an animal. I am a wild animal. When I run on trails in the wilderness, I am not suddenly faster or younger or thinner or in better shape. But I am, for some reason, exactly where I should be, doing what I want to do. The adrenaline flows faster, and there is an intensity to the concentration, an excitement in the peripheral vision.

Following behind, my husband may well have a more profound

experience. He has been on many long horse rides through the Gila National Forest and Gila Wilderness, and he knows these canyons, valleys, rivers, hills, mountains, mesas, and ridges much better than I. He sinks into places that I run through. He will remember the height of the grass and spacing of the trees and vegetation on the slopes. He will know where this canyon is in relationship to all the other folds of canyons and mountains, and he will add to that memory when he comes here next; he will compare it with what he has seen at Willow Spring or Reeds Meadow; he will nurture the growth of the living map inside him. He will build, as he has for these last twelve years, that internal geography, the imprint of land.

As for my children, who knows what patterns they see, what connections they make? We provide them with the only childhood we can, and we are sure to be surprised at the result. This afternoon, my son and daughter pass by towers of ponderosa pine, the same tree we have used for the vigas of our house, for our ceiling, for the upright beams that frame their bedroom windows. My children know to smell the inner bark of this tree for its hint of vanilla. They know that the ponderosa turns yellow only after hundreds of years. The rest of their knowledge is subterranean. They know, without knowing, the shape of the alligator juniper, the Emory oak, the Douglas fir, the narrow-leafed cottonwood. They see the forest, and they do not see it. They are not particularly quiet or receptive. They chatter, instead, about their friends and desires. They are as irreverent as squirrels.

I run until I reach the first stream crossing. It is so high that I must wade, wet to my knees, my tennis shoes soaked. The meadow starts opening up now, nearly filling the canyon bottom. The pine trees are spaced generously apart. The water courses swift and clear and purposeful, its edges meeting smoothly a thick mat of grass. It is a landscape that beckons. Run! A blue heron flaps its wings and retreats with dignity.

I think of a rancher I once talked to as we drove two hours from Reserve to Silver City. His family has been on the same public-lands ranch for a hundred years, and he feels that they have done a good job. The watershed is healthy. Wildlife is abundant. This man believes that his ranch is not an exception. He could name me "four or five families off the top of his head" who have held tight to their heritage and their love. Like Doc Hatfield, he fears that public-lands ranching may not last much longer. A dramatic increase in the federal grazing fee would drive him out of business. No one, of course, would go hungry if that happened. Both he and his wife have college educations—and he could always subdivide his private land.

Still, he says, something, something *would* go hungry. He is trying to talk about his soul.

"I didn't grow up on that ranch," he says. "It was my grandparents', and I spent my summers there. When I went back to become a rancher, I didn't know, I couldn't guess what it would come to mean to me. That kind of life. I can't describe it. But I just don't know anything that could replace it. I just don't know anything that could mean the same."

I stop for another crossing. There is no one here but me. The trees and grass glisten in the sunlight. The rock faces of the canyon move in a medley of shifting shadows. The air is alive with the constant drift of insects, pollen, and leaves. The sounds are musical: water and birds. The beauty of this place stuns me, and I lift my arms in a gesture that is not entirely conscious. I want to absorb this beauty. I want to embrace this scenery. I think about living in a ranch house at the mouth of Black Canyon—not a visitor, not on a day hike, not here for three or four or five hours. I think about *living* here, fully engaged.

"Imagine," the rancher said as we drove past Mogollon Baldy, Mud Spring Mesa, Greenwood Canyon. "Imagine what it would be like to look up at a mountain or a hill and to know that your great-grandfather also looked at that mountain and worked on it and loved it just like you do. That kind of relationship is special. I don't think our society should just throw that away."

I don't either.

I wade through the water and begin to run again.

I think of Connie Hatfield, who believes without irony that ranchers are like Native Americans, a conquered and indigenous land-based people about to lose their culture and lifestyle. "We're like those Indians now," Connie says.

I can see the irony and still empathize with Connie Hatfield.

At the same time, I will not, I cannot, relinquish my own claim to the public lands. I will not relinquish my own vision of wilderness. I will not place the needs of ranchers above my own—not those of the permittees on the Gila Wilderness, not those of that rancher in the car who spoke to me so openly and whom I liked very much. I will not place their needs above my husband's needs or my children's or my children's children or my children's children's children.

I will not place their needs above the land itself.

"I have two criteria for the solution to any problem," says Ed Chaney, a conservationist in Idaho. "Does it work? And is it honorable?"

These are the questions we must apply to the issues of wilderness preservation—and to the larger issue of grazing on our public land. We must apply them to each ecosystem, each allotment, each creekbed.

Does grazing 1,188 cows work on the Diamond Bar? Is this a sustainable agriculture? Can this area support that many cattle and still be a healthy ecosystem? Can it support that many cattle and still be considered wilderness, using our flawed definitions of the word?

We must consider the possibility that the answer is yes.

If the answer is no, we must find an honorable solution.

I run for nearly two miles until I reach Aspen Canyon. Then, as agreed, I turn back to find my family. They are not much farther along from the point where I left them. I feel energized. Something green has entered my blood. The children are completely naked and building a dam in the stream. My husband is examining grass on the bank. It's a cool season perennial that is seeding again. This year, the range will recover lushly—if the rancher takes his cows off soon.

On our way out, we go off the trail to find the ruins of a Mogollon pithouse. My son and daughter are puzzled by these circles of stone sunk into the ground. "Children like you played here a thousand years ago," my husband tells them. But a thousand years is beyond their scope.

Nothing is simple.

Two weeks after my family's hike into Black Canyon, the Forest Service range conservationist rode the same trail. He rated the condition of the stream area as poor to very poor. Oh, it was still green and grassy. But, as even ranchers know, ungrazed streams in the Southwest would normally be thick with trees and shrubs. There would be cottonwoods and willows of all age classes, young and middle-aged to replace the older giants. There would be deep, shaded, protected pools where trout could feed; there would be dense thickets of growth supporting a rich diversity of plant life and wildlife. An ungrazed stream area is not a stately parklike meadow punctuated by a single blue heron. I had been running though a garden, not a wilderness.

I knew this, of course.

Over a month later, the cows are still in Black Canyon. This certainly is not a walk I would take now. One man does and describes it in a letter to the local newspaper: "The flats surrounding the creek and canyon sides in this area were heavily grazed. The grass was cropped very short, and there were few weeds, and no shrubs or small trees left by the herd of cattle grazing. No problem, I thought, we'll just head up the canyon and soon we'll be in the 'real wilderness.' Six miles later, far above where Aspen Canyon meets Black Canyon, I was still waiting to get to the 'real wilderness.' . . . The whole canyon smelled of manure. . . . If someone had told me before I left on my hike that I would be walking up six miles of overgrazed, smelly cow pasture, I would have told them, 'Nah, no way!'"

The ranchers believe they have no choice. The cows have to go somewhere. The cows have to drink. The ranchers want stock tanks and a new management plan.

An environmentalist tells me angrily, "That area can't support any deer or wildlife now. There are no places for deer to hide or shelter."

A Forest Service official says, "Next year, when Black Canyon isn't being grazed, it'll look great again. There will be lots of grass."

"Unfortunately," he adds, "it's the trees that we really want."

At the very end of the summer, my husband also rides his horse down Black Canyon. He comes back shaken and depressed. Although this year's spring was wet, the summer rains did not come with any generosity. The cows are still in the canyon, and some areas are now completely denuded—bare, brown, eroding. It's wrong, my husband says. It's very wrong.

Is there an honorable solution? At one public meeting, the rancher on the Diamond Bar was asked if he could be "bought out" by an environmental organization.

"This is America," the man shot back. "I'll sell, if you've got enough money!"

"I don't have to *buy* out ranchers who lease public grazing rights," an environmentalist spoke up with equal heat. "I already own that land!"

Nothing is simple.

We must define our terms. We must sidestep our own prejudices and seek out the illusions wrapped in the shimmering nimbus of our words. We must also retain the power of words and the power of the dream. In the physics of beauty, we are still in the Dark Ages.

What can we do but keep looking for the light?

We tell stories.

It is an odd note, but many people concerned with range issues share the attraction for one particular story: the destruction of Africa. There are those who see its analogy here, our Great Plains its sa-

vanna, our mountain lion its tiger. These people look across the
ocean to a mystical wilderness once teeming with life, the first home
of humans colonized and looted, used up, diseased, racked, suffering,
no longer beautiful. The state director of ADC mentions the loss of
African wildlife: this is what he fears. Allan Savory laments erosion
in his native Zimbabwe. Ranchers—who know in their hearts that
they are producing *food,* a gift that is tangible, real, and important—
speak of starvation. So do those who compare the cost of raising
beef to grain. The woman from the Wilderness Society, sitting in her
Denver office, became interested in conservation as a Peace Corps
volunteer in Liberia. There, she saw too much wildland disappear for
"short-term interests." She "came back wondering, wondering what
I could do to be a world citizen."

Fear, anger, grief, love.

These emotions drive us.

4. THE GREEN WOMAN

> ❝ Culture is the key to revolution; religion is the key to culture. ❞
> —Robert Bellah

> ❝ Every day is a god, each day is a god, and holiness holds forth in time. I worship each god. I praise each day splintered down, splintered down and wrapped in time like a husk, a husk of many colors spreading, at dawn fast over the mountains split. ❞
> —Annie Dillard

WE ARE a spiritual species. The vast majority of Americans believe in God or, as the Gallup poll phrases it, "some kind of Universal Being." The vast majority of people in the world are religious. How we treat the environment around us is based on beliefs of what is sacred and what is not.

"What we do about ecology," historian Lynn White, Jr., wrote in 1967, "depends on our ideas of the man-nature relationship. More science and more technology are not going to get us out of the present ecological crisis until we find a new religion, or rethink our old one."

Traditionally, cowboys in the American West are rooted in a

Judeo-Christian heritage that places "mankind" between the animals and the angels. God is not in nature but above nature. Nature itself has no inherent value. Rather, separate parts of nature—the wolf, the cow, the lily—are assigned value by God or by humans. Made in God's image, human beings have a special place in this hierarchy of earthly creation. Earth, of course, is only a halfway house. Heaven is the goal.

In the Bible, Genesis 1:28, God blessed Adam and Eve and "said unto them, Be fruitful, and multiply, and replenish the earth, and subdue it: and have dominion over the fish of the sea and over the fowl of the air, and over every living thing that moveth upon the earth." In Genesis 9:2, God redirects Noah, "And the fear of you and the dread of you shall be upon every beast of the earth, and upon every fowl of the air, upon all that moveth upon the earth, and upon all the fishes of the sea; into your hands are they delivered."

Thus the branding iron, whip, and spur.

In cowboy literature—over a century of rhymed poetry and song—cowboys often wrote about God. An anonymous poem first published in an 1885 livestock journal celebrates the ranchers of the Old Testament:

> *Abraham emigrated in search of a range*
> *When water got scarce and he wanted a change*
> *Isaac had cattle in charge of Esau*
> *And Jacob run cows for his father-in-law*
> *He started his business clear down at bedrock*
> *And made quite a fortune by watering stock!*

Suspicious of organized religion, cowboys tended to approach their deity with wary good humor, solitarily, *mano a mano.* The subgenre of poems called "The Cowboy's Prayer" alternate from giving Him advice to asking for rain. The most common theme is thankfulness. Most cowboys took pride in the harshness of range life, but they also saw that life as extremely desirable. Cowboys were among the blessed. Prophetically, they began to mythologize themselves as soon as they rode the first long trail drive.

Poet Badger Clark wrote this classic, which he dedicated to his mother, in the early part of the twentieth century:

Oh Lord, I've never lived where churches grow.
I love creation better as it stood
The day You finished it so long ago
And looked upon Your work and called it good.
I know that others find You in the light
That's sifted down through tinted window panes,
And yet I seem to feel You near tonight
In this dim, quiet starlight on the plains.

I thank You, Lord, that I am placed so well,
That you have made my freedom so complete;
That I'm no slave of whistle, clock, or bell,
Nor weak-eyed prisoner of wall and street.
Just let me live my life as I've begun
And give me work that's open to the sky;
Make me a pardner of the wind and sun,
And I won't ask a life that's soft or high.

Let me be easy on the man that's down;
Let me be square and generous with all.
I'm careless sometimes, Lord, when I'm in town,
But never let 'em say I'm mean or small!
Make me as big and open as the plains,
As honest as the hoss between my knees
Clean as the wind that blows behind the rains,
Free as the hawk that circles down the breeze!

Forgive me, Lord, if I sometimes forget.
You know about the reasons that are hid.
You understand the things that gall and fret;

> You know me better than my mother did.
> Just keep an eye on all that's done and said,
> And right me, sometimes, when I turn aside,
> And guide me on the long, dim trail ahead
> That stretches upward toward the Great Divide.

Cowboy poetry is a folk art that continues to thrive. Each year, any number of cowboy poetry readings or "gatherings," as they are called, take place in the West. One of these, in my town of Silver City, included an open session for amateurs called "Sky Ranch." Bravely, men and women got up to face the crowd and talk about God. These were local people: a Mimbres cowboy, a Baptist preacher, a lineman for the telephone company.

Tongue-in-cheek, rancher Dick Hays had this to say about Heaven:

> There's a land above the stars,
> Far above the Milky Way,
> Where cattle roam in thousands
> And cutting horses play.
>
> There ain't no jigger bosses
> To tell yuh what to do,
> Saint Peter turns yuh loose
> And leaves it up to you.
>
> They've sent the alkali and loco
> To the devil down below,
> And filaria and grama grass
> On all the ridges grow.
>
> There ain't no blasted bird hunter
> A-shootin' in the draw,
> And single riggin' saddles
> Is strict against the law.

There ain't no rattlesnakes a-rattlin'
On all the high divides,
There ain't no water like the Pecos
To eat up yer insides.

There ain't no crooked cow buyers
Fulla lowlifed tricks,
And there ain't no such thing
As lice, er scab, er ticks.

There ain't no politicians
With their three-fer-dime cigars
She's a land of peace and quiet
Up there above the stars.

No loco weed, no ticks, no politicians.

This is a God who willingly excludes species that are bad for cows. He is a personalized male you can talk to as you ride in the saddle. He is the Creator who looked down on His finished work a long time ago. He is the God who rejected Cain, a tiller of the ground, and accepted Abel, a keeper of sheep.

Over the last thirty years, He has also been accused of being sexist, dualistic, static, and ecologically unsound.

In an article that would be anthologized many times, Lynn White, Jr., complained that the Judeo-Christian tradition "not only established a dualism of man and nature but also insisted that it is God's will that man exploit nature for his proper ends." When Christianity triumphed over paganism, "the spirits *in* nature, which formerly had protected nature from man, evaporated." There were no more sacred groves; there was only lumber to harvest. Rivers could be dammed without thought, mountains mined, species exterminated. The conquest of nature became a religious quest for Christian scientists from

Friar Roger Bacon to Isaac Newton. In the mid-nineteenth century, science and technology combined to create the potential for planet-wide destruction. Christianity provided the philosophical framework. And "Christianity," White declared, "bears a huge burden of guilt."

People had said this before—but never so boldly.

Not everyone agreed.

Some argued that many, different factors played a role in the western use of natural resources. They pointed to other major civilizations controlled by other major religions that were equally wasteful and destructive. Biblical scholars protested that the "subdue and dominate" speech was being misinterpreted, another, closer reading of the Bible emphasized harmony and stewardship. Defenders of Christianity found themselves returning to the oldest roots of the Jewish tradition, to the mystical literature of Israel: the Psalms, the Song of Songs, the books of Proverbs, Sirach, Ecclesiastes, and Job. Some felt that the intense spirituality of the Old Testament in regard to nature could hardly be understood today; our own categorized thinking was "an ironic stumbling block."

Other theologians took up the challenge to find an alternative view—a Christian ecotheology.

They often began by rejecting the religion's basic cultural context. Jay McDaniel, a professor of religion, says that "patriarchy has been at the root of Christian and Western insensitivity to the natural world" and "in the mythical heritage of Christianity, the rights of nonhuman nature have been disregarded, sexuality has been desacralized, and women (often identified with nature and sexuality) have been victimized."

McDaniel is also concerned with the rights of animals and concludes, "For many of us, an ecological spirituality will rightly lead to the adoption of a vegetarian diet."

Feminist Penelope Washbourn urges a return to the wisdom of the human body. She asks Christians to more fully explore the female cycle of menstruation, intercourse, orgasm, conception, pregnancy, birth, lactation, and menopause.

Sallie McFague writes about a new marriage of science and religion. "For the first time in several hundred years we have the possibility of thinking holistically about God and the world, and this possibility is being given to us by the 'common creation story' coming from the sciences, from cosmology, astrophysics, and biology. . . . To feel that we belong to the earth and to accept our proper place within it is the beginning of a natural piety."

The well known philosopher John B. Cobb, Jr., rejects enlightened self-interest for a self-transcendent Christian love that sees the rest of Creation as having "some intrinsic right to exist and prosper."

Feminist theology, ecofeminism, ecological spirituality, process theology: this was new growth on a very old tree.

In the greening of Christianity, few are more radical than Matthew Fox, who entered the Dominican order in his late teens. Fox's *Original Blessing,* was published in 1986 and *The Coming of the Cosmic Christ* in 1988. In response, the Vatican ordered the priest to stop speaking and writing publicly for a year. Matthew Fox agreed. Soon after the year was over, he brought forth *Creation Spirituality: Liberating Gifts for the Peoples of the Earth.*

The cover of this book uses the Celtic image of God as a feminine trinity. The Virgin, a black woman in African dress, has just given birth to a globe of the earth still attached to her by its umbilical cord. The Mother, middle-aged and vaguely Middle Eastern, kneels on the Virgin's left to support the globe. A Crone representing death stands on the Virgin's right. This woman is clearly from a Plains tribe in North America. A buffalo decorates her buckskin robe. A black raven flaps at her feet. Encompassing the three figures is a patterned snake eating its own tail.

Inside, Fox writes that creation spirituality "begins with creation and the cosmos. Only later does it get to the human story, which then attracts us like a jewel set in the larger drama of creation itself." Creation spirituality "empowers us for an ecological era, a time when we cease looking *up* for divinity and start looking *around*." Creation spirituality is the heritage of most native cultures that "expect the divine to burst out of anyplace at anytime." Creation spirituality is feminist, mystic, panentheistic, and profoundly ecumenical. It celebrates our natural diversity. Why, for example, "should a heterosexual be threatened by a homosexual or vice versa?" Fox wonders. "Vive la différence!" Creation spirituality is a path for social justice in the First World just as liberation theology is a path for the Third World. Creation spirituality could even free "Roman Catholicism from its flirtations with fascism in this century."

One can see, perhaps, what was bothering the Vatican.

According to Fox, a main complaint was that he called God "Mother" in *Original Blessing*. He showed that many early mystics did the same: influential women, such as Hildegard of Bingen and Julian of Norwich, who were neglected and persecuted by the Church. These mystics celebrated the blessing of God's creation, not the self-loathing and contempt of original sin.

"See! I am God!" shouted Julian of Norwich in the twelfth century. "See! I am in everything. See! I never lift my hands off my work, nor will I ever. See! I lead everything toward the purpose for which I ordained it, without beginning, by the same Power, Wisdom and Love by which I created it. How could anything be amiss?"

More specifically, "When I speak of 'original blessing,'" Fox writes, "I am speaking of those blessings of healthy soil, living forests, clean waters, and healthy DNA in our reproductive systems. These blessings form the basis of a true living economy—they constitute our essential wealth."

Matthew Fox is haunted by a dream he had on March 15, 1986. It climaxed with the refrain, "Your mother is dying."

"We have begun to put our hands in her lanced side and in her crucified hands and feet. . . . Matricide—the killing of the mother principle—is being committed against Mother Earth, mother brain and mother creativity; against mother religions and mother wisdom, against youth; against mother church, mother compassion and fatherhood as well."

The quest today is for the Cosmic Christ and a living cosmology that includes science (the source of a new creation story), mysticism (psychic union with the mysteries of creation), and art (expressions of awe at creation). Jesus is someone we must reclaim as the "pattern that connects" offered to us in the form of a particular historical person. Our science classes already affirm that all things *are* connected, from the spiral crab nebula to the genes of a crayfish. In addition, Fox urges spiritual "laboratories in painting, clay, ritual, massage, and music to teach the art of mystical development. Churches and synagogues require laboratories of prayer where the 'prune brain' that the right lobe has become can be watered, nourished, and developed."

To reclaim the Cosmic Christ requires a paradigm shift. It begins when we discover a problem or phenomenon for which our worldview is inadequate. Fox believes that "the war on nature and Mother Earth" is such a problem. The result is crisis and breakdown. Out of this, a new worldview—a new mythology—can emerge.

For Matthew Fox, creation is unfolding, right now, here in the present. It is not a done deed. This, too, is part of the prophetic tradition of the Jewish Bible and New Testament, where God is experienced as one who calls humanity forward and stimulates change.

Jay McDaniel writes that in the last five hundred years "rarely has the essence of Christianity itself been construed as an ongoing process—a process in which Christians are invited to be open to possibilities for new vision." McDaniel believes that change requires both remembrance and repentance. Remembrance is an acknowledgment of the past, good and bad. Repentance is a "transformation lured by the image of how life can be lived in the future."

The Coming of the Cosmic Christ has a subtitle: *The Healing of Mother Earth and the Birth of a Global Renaissance.*

Matthew Fox prophesizes change on a large scale.

"Who would dare to speak of a renaissance in our times?" he asks. "Is it a bourgeois dream of an armchair theologian, a romantic cop-out from an academician? Who in their right mind would look at the suffering in today's world and suggest that the human race is, in fact, on the verge of a vast global renaissance? I suppose it is the mystic in me that dares to suggest such a vision. And why? Because the mystic teaches us to trust all bottomless out, all emptying, all nothingness experiences as the matrix and patrix of new birth. It is precisely the despair of our times that convinces me that a renaissance is right around the corner, that a renaissance is the only answer to the depths of our dilemma. It is either renaissance or planetary extinction. There is no middle ground."

"For God so loved the world," says the New Testament, "that He gave it His only begotten Son."

Perhaps the word *world* was used for good reason.

"Walking, I am listening to a deeper way. Suddenly all my ancestors are behind me. Be still, they say. Watch and listen. You are the results of the love of thousands."
—*Chickasaw poet Linda Hogan*

In 1500 some six to twelve million Native Americans probably inhabited the United States; by 1890, their population had been reduced to 250,000, partly due to warfare but mainly because of diseases brought by invading Europeans. In 1990, the U.S. Census

Bureau reported 2 million Native Americans, Eskimos, and Aleuts, with more than half of these still living on their tribal lands. The rest had moved off the reservation but usually stayed close enough to visit relatives and return for ceremonials. Indian reservations total over fifty-two million acres, ranging from small rancherias in California to the fifteen-million-acre Navajo Nation. There are more than three hundred tribes in this country. Their right to exist in sovereign and culturally distinct ways is guaranteed by nearly four hundred treaties and many, many legal agreements.

The religious traditions of Native Americans in the West are not relics from the past. They were at the heart of cultures still intact and unassimilated a hundred years ago. They are at the heart of cultures still living today. The feasts and corn dances at the nineteen pueblos of New Mexico are not for tourists; they are community acts of worship. Somewhere, an Apache dresses for her puberty ceremony. A Navajo tells the story of Changing Woman. A Tewa is blossoming into a "finished person." A Pawnee uses tobacco in a peyote ritual. A Blackfeet starts the Sun Dance. A Lummi passes a feather. An Arapaho kills a fish. A Papago gathers saguaro fruit.

Native Americans are an extremely diverse group. They came to this continent in waves of migration, perhaps separated from each other by as much as twelve thousand years. They speak different languages, and they were shaped by different patterns of weather and geography. Still, most Native Americans agree on certain similarities in their relationship to the land.

"We are the land," writes Paula Gunn Allen, of Laguna and Lebanese descent. "To the best of my understanding, that is the fundamental idea embedded in Native American life and culture in the Southwest. More than remembered, the earth is the mind of the people as we are the mind of the earth."

"The American Indian," says N. Scott Momaday, half Kiowa and half Cherokee, "has a very long experience of the North American continent, going back thousands of years, maybe thirty thousand. So

I think of that as being a very great investment, a kind of spiritual investment in the landscape."

"The Indian lives with his land," explained Vine Deloria, Jr., a Standing Rock Sioux. "He feared to destroy it by changing its natural shape because he realized that it was more than a useful tool for exploitation. It sustained all life, and without other forms of life, man himself could not survive. People used to laugh at the Indian respect for smaller animals. Indians called them little brother. The Plains Indians appeased the buffalo after they had slain them for food. They well understood that without all life respecting itself and each other no society could indefinitely maintain itself."

Landscape becomes particularly important when religious mythology is wrapped around particular lakes and rivers and mountains. For many tribes, the story of creation happened right here, in the American West. For the Papago, life on this earth began at Mount Baboquivari in southeastern Arizona. The first generations of the Nez Perce grew up at two places, Kakayohneme Creek and Tannish, fifteen miles above the mouth of Little Salmon River. The creator Usen gave Geronimo's people a very specific homeland in what is now the Gila Wilderness. The Oglala believe that "first man sprang from the soil in the midst of the great plains." The Navajos are surrounded by sacred mountains brought up from the underworld; we know them as Blanca Peak, Mount Taylor, San Francisco Peaks, Herperus Peak, Huerfano Mountain, and Gobernador Knob.

The earth is the mind of the people.

A number of tribes also use landscape as a way of teaching social values. Working with the Apaches who live near Cibeque, Arizona, anthropologist Keith Basso recorded some of their stories in his book *Western Apache Language and Culture*. These stories begin with the description of an actual physical place.

"It happened at coarse-textured-rocks-lie-above-in-a-compact-cluster" tells of a man who sexually molests his stepdaughter. The girl's uncle kills the offender and drags him to coarse-textured-rocks-lie-above-in-a-compact-cluster. To emphasize their abhorrence of incest, the relatives never have a wake for the man's body.

"It happened at big-cottonwood-trees-stand-spreading-here-and-there" goes back to a time when the Apaches and Pimas were at war. Custom dictates that mothers do not interfere with their daughter's husbands. But in the night, an old woman wakes and loudly chastises her son-in-law. The Pimas, coincidentally, are raiding the village. They run to the old woman's camp and kill her. This story is about the danger of overstepping traditional social roles.

"It happened at men-stand-above-here-and-there" concerns an Apache policeman who catches another Apache killing a white man's cow. When the officer tries to inform his superiors, his mind is befuddled by witchcraft. The policeman is the butt of this joke; he is behaving too much like a white man himself.

In 1977, Keith Basso was at a party at which the story "it happened at men-stand-above-here-and-there" is told to an Apache teenager who had recently worn plastic curlers at a girl's puberty ceremony. The girl leaves the party abruptly. The grandmother, who has reprimanded her with this story, explains, "I shot her with an arrow." Years later, the girl and the anthropologist are together in a car. They pass by *ndee dah naaziih* (men-stand-above-here-and-there) and the girl smiles, speaking in Apache. "I know that place. It stalks me every day."

Apache Nick Thompson says, "It's hard to keep living right. Many things jump at you and block your way. But you won't forget that story. You're going to see the place where it happened, maybe every day if it's nearby and close to Cibeque. If you don't see it, you're going to hear its name and see it in your mind. It doesn't matter if you get old—that place will keep stalking you like the one who shot you with the story."

Keith Basso writes that after the storyteller begins the process: "Mountains and arroyos step in symbolically for grandmothers and uncles. . . . Losing the land is something the Western Apache can ill afford to do, for geographical features have served the people for centuries as indispensable mnemonic pegs on which to hang the moral teachings of their history."

We are the land.

We are the mind of the earth.

We are part of nature and dependent on nature.

A society that believes this will provide social controls that prevent its members from disrupting the natural balance. These controls are imperfect. Native Americans can and do overuse their resources. Many examples—the use of jumps for antelope and buffalo, the overgrazing of the Navajo and Papago reservations—remind us not to simplify. Still, we do not need to idealize native cultures in order to agree with Matthew Fox that they offer an important worldview.

For Native Americans, the problem is how to keep their world and its view alive.

For non-Indians, the question is how to approach the cosmology of another culture. The psychologist Carl Jung once warned his colleagues, enamored with the myths of Asia, that they "could not take on the gorgeous trappings of the Orient." So, too, most Americans cannot chant the Blessing Way or go on a vision quest or understand, remotely, the power of a pendant of abalone shell.

Writer Leslie Marmon Silko—Laguna, Hispanic, and Anglo—speaks sharply of "the assumption that the white man, through some innate cultural or racial superiority, has the ability to perceive and master the essential beliefs, values, and emotions of persons from Native American communities."

The poet Linda Hogan, half Chickasaw, is more gentle with her non-Indian students who long "for something they believe existed in earlier times or in tribal people. What they want is their own life, their own love for the earth, but when they speak their own words about it, they don't believe them, so they look to Indians, forgetting that enlightenment can't be found in a weekend workshop, forgetting that most Indian people are living the crisis of American life, the toxins of chemical waste, the pain of what is repressed in white America. There is not such a thing as becoming an instant shaman, an instant healer, an instantly spiritualized person. Instant coffee is more likely."

Tito Naranjo is a Tewa Indian from the Santa Clara Pueblo in northern New Mexico. Tito also speaks, with concern, about the importance of context.

"Language is the key," he says. "Tewa words are laden with meaning."

Tito Naranjo stops, thinks, starts again, fumbles. This is not easy. He recites, suddenly, a string of Tewa words.

"That brings everything back up for me," he says. "I wish I could put that in your head and you could understand that. Then you could pull it apart and explain it. But to reach this place, this entire universe that I have inside, takes a base of information, lots of information. A way of life occurs in context, physical and cultural context, the context of language."

"The word *water*," Tito tries, "is not just a product that we use on a daily basis. Socially, in the Tewa story of creation, we emerged from water. We *are* water. We *are* the water. We are the *nature* of water, in spirit, in our origin. That's the reality that is passed on in the Tewa culture. . . . In the name bear, the name for bear, is the understanding that he is my brother, my younger brother, my older brother. If the bear is my kin, how can I wipe him out? How can I live without the bear? In the Pueblo world, these ideas are not only in your head. They are in your heart, your whole being."

During the 1940s, when Tito was growing up in Santa Clara, he thought that the Pueblo world would always remain the same.

"Every day was connected to the land," he says, "to the dirt, to prayer. It was seamless. It's hard to pull out any special moment. You'd see old men going up to the mesa tops to pray. You'd have cornmeal in your hands. Every day was tied to water, to mountains, to clouds. When you talked about clouds, you talked about supernaturals. When you talked about corn, you talked about the essence of life. This was a *rich* way of life. It was absolutely satisfying. It was self-contained. This was my reality and I thought that reality would go on forever. I thought: when I grow up, I'm going to raise corn. When I grow up, I'm going to have horses. When I grow up, I'm going to plow."

In 1940, the scientific laboratory Los Alamos was built 18 miles south of Santa Clara in the foothills of the Jemez Mountains. Many Tewa went there to work for wages. World War II came, and many more Native Americans went to war. The self-contained Pueblo world began to seriously fracture. Like Native Americans across the West, Pueblo children were still being educated in day schools and boarding schools run by the Bureau of Indian Affairs. The point of this education was assimilation into the white world; the process was brutal.

"Change is a given," Tito says today. "No society has ever stayed the same. But that other world didn't tell me that. There was this other way, this continuity, and then there was this absolute discontinuity! In the pits, in the chasm, in the gorge! There is an agony, and sometimes it is the agony of defeat. . . . For forty years I was in anguish and anxiety, making that transition, crossing the line of acculturation. It began sharply when I was a teenager. The price is great. . . . I am two people now. I am acculturated. And I am this other, this Tewa man, too."

Tito Naranjo, his eight sisters, and his one brother have a large collection of college degrees. They went out into the white world as architects, poets, sculptors, potters, and professors. They are, in American terms, a success.

Not every Native American can say the same. Unemployment on many reservations is in excess of 50 percent; 45 percent of reservation Indians live below the poverty line. As a group, Native Ameri-

cans are the poorest in this country and suffer significantly from al-
coholism, suicide, disease, and malnutrition.

Conquest has brought more subtle losses as well. Paula Gunn Allen believes that acculturation slam-dunked many southwestern Indians from women-centered cultures into a society that was sexist,
sexually repressed, materialistic, and homophobic. "The loss of status
is so great," she says. "It's so great I can barely begin to talk about
it."

In Tito's own pueblo, children of full-blooded Santa Clara women
who marry non–Santa Clara men are denied tribal membership.
Lineage is traced only through the male, and women have become
"second-class citizens."

Yet this is a worldview that includes major female deities, the
White Corn Mother and Blue Corn Mother, who guided the people from the underworld and nurtured them in their transition to
this realm. The concept of *gia*, or mother, is used to identify "ideal
beingness." *Gia* is another word laden with meaning—a word that
operates on many levels. As well as referring to the biological
mother, *gia* is used to address the earth, supernaturals, and religious
symbols; important community leaders; and important figures within
the extended family. The ideal leader or *cacique* of the Pueblo is
called a "woman-man" or *nung be gia*.

"The *gia* concept shows that women in the traditional setting
were predominant and of primary importance in all areas of Pueblo
life," Tito once wrote for a scholarly journal. "But those *gia* qualities of nurturing, encompassing, loving, giving and caring are no
longer the directive ideals which molded the traditional Santa Clara
community."

In 1962, out of college, Tito married a woman from the Taos
Pueblo, and they traveled. They went to graduate school. They went
to Utah. They went to Alaska. At some point they decided not to return to live in a pueblo. Instead, they bought one hundred acres in
a small rural valley some forty miles from both Taos and Santa Clara.

They chose to propel their children into the world of change. They chose to continue forward, through transition.

They have their doubts. Tito's two sons do not speak Tewa, and he has to wonder what the word *water* or *bear* means to them. "They know that they are Indian," Tito says. "And that's about all they know. My biggest desire, now, is to leave them something they can remember, a thread, some connection back to the world they genetically come from."

The Naranjos still live in that small valley, a place not unlike the place where I live—increasingly open to development and less isolated every year. This is high country, rugged and forested with pine and Douglas fir. Rivers run swiftly in the spring. Turkey and deer lead secret lives. Bears prowl the bush. Bluejay scream alarm.

Tito loves this land.

And the "sharpest cultural double bind" he experiences is the gap between the Pueblo view of land and the American way.

"The Pueblo world tells me that I belong here forever and ever," Tito says. "I belong right here, down underneath. I return here. I don't go to Heaven or Hell. But this other American world is telling me that I don't belong here! To come from a culture that absolutely says that you belong to the earth, it's yours, forever, and then for this other culture to say that you don't, you don't . . . "

Discontinuity has many edges. For Native Americans, memories of broken treaties and promises are still painful. They mourn for what they had and for what was taken away. All over the West, the religious map that indigenous people made of the land clashes with non-Indian ideas of ownership.

Four miles from Huerfano Mountain, where the Navajos' earliest ancestors emerged, an insulation company tries to put an asbestos waste dump on private property. "That's like burying hazardous waste in the front lawn of a local church," says the Navajo Nation president. A woman explains to a newspaper reporter, "Environment, health, and religion are not isolated issues for the Navajo people.

They are all meshed together in our culture. Our land is all we have, and our beliefs and way of life depend on the land."

In Montana, the Forest Service leases the drainages of the Badger and Two Medicine Rivers for oil and gas exploration. The Blackfeet say that drilling will disrupt their use of sacred sites. They are reluctant to explain, exactly, where these sites are.

A butte fifty miles outside the Hopi reservation is the southern boundary of the homeland the Hopis once knew. Each year, leaders come to lay prayer feathers before a three-foot-high marker set up generations ago in a pact with Masau, the creator of the Hopi world. In 1991, the marker was bulldozed by a gravel mining company.

Indian groups point to at least fifteen sacred areas that have been, or are, in danger. These include the Crazy Mountains in Montana, Mount Hood in Oregon, Mount Shasta in California, the Black Hills in South Dakota, the Rainbow Bridge in Arizona, and the Hawaii Volcanoes National Park.

Non-Indians have more than an obligation in this; we have an interest. If we care about the land, we must nurture all people who care about the land and all forms of caring. We must imagine a West that is truly culturally and biologically diverse, "a pattern that connects," rich in our mutual resources.

Environmentalists often are allies with Native Americans against the demand to drill for oil or dump toxic wastes or set up a missile range. But, in other cases, the same environmentalists may not understand a culture that desires to subsist on the land—to graze sheep and cattle, trap wild animals, and gather plants.

Significantly, there are times when the environmentalist and the Native American and the rancher all want the same piece of land. The Sandia Pueblo, for example, say that a faulty 1859 survey cheated them out of 8,800 acres that are now in the Cibola National Forest and Sandia Wilderness Area; the Acomas lay claim to much of the El Malpais National Monument and Conservation Area; the Western Shoshones want back BLM land in Nevada. These struggles are not easily resolved.

"My own lifeway, the Pueblo worldview, is religious," Tito says. "The environmental movement . . . is intellectual. They both teach us to be circumspect. On my land here I know I am sitting on a Precambrian shelf that is bringing up water. I will go see a specialist before I put in an outhouse. I am being circumspect, intellectually. To do that religiously is something else. It is to protect everything to the ultimate. . . . One way is testable. We can measure pollutants. The other way is untestable."

At one point, as Tito speaks, his wife returns from teaching special education at a local high school. Bernice Naranjo is an energetic, effervescent, warm-hearted woman. She was eighteen when she married Tito and left the Taos Pueblo where she was born. She contrasts with and complements her husband. Together, they show the range of Native American experience.

"My philosophy is very modern," Bernice laughs. As well as a teacher, she is a traditional potter in both the Taos and Santa Clara style. "But I don't see myself as a traditional Indian. I love computers, robotics, modern life. I don't feel that I need to bless the earth or to use prayer feathers when I make pots. I have my own view. . . . "

Bernice says that she became a potter by "reading a book." She isn't comfortable dancing at the Taos ceremonials. Sometimes she feels like an alien there. Like Tito's family, she and her sisters have all gone to graduate school. Bernice likes her job as a special education teacher. She looks at me and sees someone who is more similar than different. We are both women, after all. We are both mothers. We worry about the same things. She sees a commonality.

In the grace of marital balance, she and Tito form a whole.

She concludes by returning to what is central, to the heart and the core. "Tito and I share basic values," Bernice Naranjo says definitely. "We share a sense of what is sacred."

In two days, Tito and Bernice's father will perform in the spring relay races at the Taos Pueblo. "We will walk into the kiva," Tito says. "The first time I did this I realized, at that moment, that I was all Pueblo. This was absolutely and completely how it had been before the Spanish came. There was no other world but this world of being a Pueblo Indian." The races themselves are not about competition. "They are about nurturing the sun on its summer journey," Tito explains. "In September, again, the Taos Pueblo will send the sun on its winter journey. If the Taos Pueblo did not do this, the sun would extinguish. It would die."

Tito Naranjo's father-in-law has spent as long as forty days in the kiva. For eighteen months at a time, he helps train young men in a lifestyle that declares, unambiguously, that the earth is the mind of the people and the people the mind of the earth.

In our visions of the future, in the future of the West, we cannot forget the importance of the Taos Pueblo.

Tito's sister, Rina Swentzell, is an architect and adviser to the Museum of Indian Arts and Culture in Santa Fe. She speaks to an audience of Anglos, Native Americans, and Hispanics. "We are born literally from the womb of the Mother. As the people move out of the underworld, born out of the earth, that connection is so incredible! When we are asked to talk about the connection between land and the people, between people and the natural environment, how can we talk about it except to say that it is so intimate? Think of children. How can children . . . how can I say of my mother that I don't belong to her?"

At Cibeque, the Apache girl bounces lightly, first on one foot and then on another. The power of Changing Woman enters her body. As Changing Woman kneels, the rays of the sun shine into the place where she will later bleed for the first time.

In Montana, at the Sun Dance, a Blackfeet woman of good health and character stands to make the vows on behalf of her people. The ground and water surrounding her must be absolutely clean and without blemish. There can be no illness in the land, no contamination.

At the Santa Clara Pueblo, the Tewa who has blossomed into a "finished person" goes for a walk. He sees a stone and picks it up.

With cupped hands, he brings the rock past his mouth and inhales the air. Then he puts the stone back. "Thank you," he says. "You have shared your spirit and life with me today."

"Re-inhabitory refers to the tiny number of persons who come out of the industrial societies (having collected or squandered the fruits of 8,000 years of civilization) and then start to turn back to the land, to place. This comes for some with the rational and scientific realization of inter-connectedness, and planetary limits. But the actual demands of a life committed to a place, and living somewhat by the sunshine green plant energy that is concentrating in that spot, are so physically and intellectually intense, that it is a moral and spiritual choice as well."
—*Gary Snyder*

In New Mexico, Tito Naranjo helped his father with the corn. He was six years old. The rhythms of the pueblo were like a pulse of blood, moving from his heart, to his arms, to his heart again. At about the same time, Peter Berg was also six years old and traveling on a train from New York to Florida, a state where his mother, a "strong, proto-liberated woman," could get an easy divorce. Peter was dressed in a little sailor suit, World War II style, when he woke in the Jacksonville trainyard to see palm trees floating by the window. He stared in amazement. He had never seen such a thing in his life! It dawned on him then that he was in a very new place—an entirely new geography. Soon he would be a Yankee going to school in the South, thrust into a culture he didn't understand, into a world of strange plants and trees and birds and animals, of Seminoles and alligators and spoonbill cranes.

"It became a very serious matter," Peter says now, "for me to try and find out *where I was.*"

Peter Berg is obsessed with the idea of place. He wants to know the difference between what is tourist and what is native, between passing through and living.

"Inauthenticity is the real rat that gnaws at the soul," he says.

"Growing up in Florida and looking for reality . . . " he muses.

He could be talking about many Americans, who usually start looking for reality by looking somewhere else. Peter tried that: Mexico, Europe, Canada. In the early 1960s, he finally rumbled into the San Francisco Bay Area on a lumber freight train. Soon he was writing, directing, and acting in the San Francisco Mime Troupe; with others, he took "guerilla theater" into the streets of Haight-Ashbury and helped form the Diggers, a self-proclaimed "experiment in human ecology," anarchistic and idealistic, passing out food to the poor and finding shelter for the flower children. The Diggers had social and political concerns. They also knew that cities were built out of natural resources, that these resources came from somewhere, and that these resources were not infinite. They knew that people ate soil and sun. They believed in the weed cracking the sidewalk.

In 1962, Rachel Carson's book on pesticides, *Silent Spring,* became a best-seller. Like *Uncle Tom's Cabin* and Harriet Beecher Stowe ("the little lady who started the big war"), Carson served as the catalyst for a shift in cultural ethics. In American thought, the foundations for "the age of ecology" already had been laid by Whitman, Emerson, Thoreau, Muir, Jeffers, Leopold, and others. In the 1960s, the song swelled with authors such as Gary Snyder and Alan Watts. Historian Lynn White, Jr., questioned Christianity. Economist E. F. Schumacher questioned unlimited growth. Scientists, particularly physicists, spoke in mystical terms. The first Earth Day was held in 1970. The environmental movement was born.

Peter Berg and his partner, Judy Goldhaft, began a tour of alternative, land-based communes. They made a video of their journey, adding to the film as each place told its story. The project took them from California to Maine, from sexual liberation communities to alternative energy farms, from Yogis to Weathermen. It was a crash course. What's working. What's not.

"These were communal people," Judy Goldhaft says. "They grew their own food. They had their babies at home. They didn't want to be involved in industrial society. Yet everywhere we went, the farthest out in the country we could go, there was some environmental catastrophe to deal with, a nuclear power plant, the government spraying toxic defoliants, DDT in the water."

In mid-winter, at kitchen table discussions, Peter and Judy heard the word *bioregion* for the first time. Taken from German texts on natural science, a bioregion was a closely connected web of native plants, animals, and geography—a watershed or a distinct area like the Mojave Desert. By deliberate omission, the term did not include the human species.

In 1972, Peter went to the first United Nations Conference on the Environment. He spent his time in the streets videotaping the thousands of people who came to the conference but were not allowed to participate. He left believing that there had to be a different approach, something "that was not nation-state oriented." He came to believe that this approach should be *bioregional,* with *bioregion* expanded to encompass *Homo sapiens*. People who thought bioregionally would base their culture and economy on what was sustainable in the area where they lived. The ecology of each bioregion would become the lens through which all human activity could be viewed.

We might be saved yet by a strong sense of place.

This was a thought to take home, back to San Francisco. This was a thought you might find yourself thinking the rest of your life.

Judy Goldhaft was raised in southern New Jersey, on the edge of the Pine Barrens, a rural area that provided produce for Philadelphia and

New York City. As a child, she roamed the countryside, solitarily, poetically, her senses wide open. She knew the names of the things around her; she knew exactly where she was. At the age of twenty-one, when she moved to northern California with her first husband, the shock was as great as Peter's epiphany of floating palm trees. The need was as great too. *What was that bird over there, and what was it eating?*

A dancer, with a degree in philosophy, Judy also became part of the Diggers and San Francisco Mime Troupe. She remembers taking a workshop in which the instructor called out inspirational topics. These were ideas that Judy Goldhaft had been told were undanceable. She had been told you couldn't move to words such as *socialism* or *grass*. She found that she could. She found that theater could do a lot of things, that it could return straight to ritual: celebrating "planetary holidays" such as the summer solstice, bringing the outside in. Soon Judy was handing out great leafy branches to her own audiences, telling them that they, too, could dance.

When she and Peter returned to San Francisco, Judy took the word *bioregion* and put it into theater. She researched the stories of humans indigenous to northern California, the Pomo and Karok, the Miwok. Many of these stories included other species: Bluejay, Badger, Mole, and Grizzly. They were biocentric tales. They were bawdy. They were grounded in a very specific knowledge of what to eat and where to find it. They became the basis for scripts that had Lizard and Coyote exchanging puns, competitively comparing lifestyles, and debating, acrimoniously, whether humans should have hands.

Lizard was all for it.

"Hands like mine," he rhapsodized. "Human beings will have hands. They'll want to scramble up rock piles. . . . "

Coyote demurred. "No, they won't. Human beings will have paws . . . furry knuckles are sexier. . . . Besides, humans are too dangerous. They'll have your ass if you give 'em hands, Liz."

"Oh, we had some wonderful moments," Judy says. "We didn't use costumes or masks. Instead we had to really learn about animals, their behavioral movements, their nonverbal communication. We'd go out in the country somewhere and perform a creation story where Silver Fox and Coyote made the world by singing, and the local dogs would recognize the canine body language and go crazy, rushing up to the stage."

Of the entire bioregional movement, poet Gary Snyder said, "We are doing not street theatre now but mountain, river, and field theatre. We present a larger vision than most people have been willing to permit themselves."

Meanwhile Peter Berg was writing an essay called "Strategies for Reinhabiting the Northern California Bioregion," which he would later revise with Raymond F. Dasmann. The authors contrasted a society that "lives in place" with one that destructively "makes a living" from the land. They defined reinhabitation as "learning to live-in-place in an area that has been disrupted and injured through past exploitation." They pointed to the original inhabitants of California, who had kept the land relatively healthy for at least fifteen thousand years, and noted that "reinhabitants are as different from invaders as these were from the original inhabitants. . . . Their most basic goals are to restore and maintain watersheds, topsoil, and native species, elements of obvious necessity for in-place existence."

Reinhabitation leads to a simple but radically un-American idea: don't move. Get to know a place, commit to a place, love a place, protect a place, become part of the biological and social community of a place—and then stay there. Peter Berg says that, on the average, Americans change their addresses every three years. When people stay in place, however, they create a social power base that can be extremely effective. (This surely accounts for some of the authority we have given to Anglo ranchers in the West.)

In their house in the Mission District of San Francisco, Peter and Judy began to publicize these ideas. They printed and distributed "bundles" of information: maps, booklets, and poems that focused on a particular bioregion. They formed the educational Planet Drum Foundation in 1974 and the newsletter "Raise the Stakes" in 1979. By 1992, there were more than 250 bioregional groups and publications in North America and any number of conferences.

Bioregionalism is not, obviously, a household word. In the environmental community, its proponents do not compare with the membership of the Sierra Club or National Wildlife Federation. Nor do Peter and Judy link themselves to such mainstream groups. Like some others, Peter believes that the creation of the Environmental Protection Agency in 1973 ended a period of broad, grassroots volunteerism; the movement became a branch of the legal profession. No one, he says, "can doubt the moral basis of environmentalism." Still, he finds the whole thing oddly defensive, negative, reactive, and, yes, co-opted by business and industrial interests.

As early as the nineteenth century, environmentalists began to divide into two camps: those who favored management and those who celebrated pure preservation. A hundred years later, the division is more complex.

Believers in a "deep ecology" see shallow or "reform environmentalism" as too limited and anthropocentric. The very word *environment* seems to draw a line between humans and nature. Ecology, however, is a concept that forms a circle, with humanity very much inside that circle, right beside the grizzly bear and fringe toed lizard. Deep ecologists seriously question the tenets of this Late Industrial Age: centralized political structures, infinite economic growth, consumerism, and a naive reliance on high-tech solutions. Environmentalists seek mainly to reform, not to challenge, these ideas. They hope only to soften the blow.

Much of this is the natural splintering of any movement. Most people working on environmental issues are unique amalgams, both shallow and deep, conservative and radical.

Still, a real distinction between the two philosophies may lie in the difference between what is "intuitive" and what is—as Tito Naranjo says—"intellectual." Deep ecology involves personal transformation. It takes the scientific understanding that "everything is connected" and gives that a spiritual dimension. This is particularly welcome to those Americans who have no cultural context for worship, who would not be comfortable in a church or a kiva or a synagogue. It is useful to those who were brought up in schools where knowledge is deliberately separated from prayer and where the pursuit of information is the highest ambition. Deep ecology may begin as information. But it can deepen to a religious view not so dissimilar to that of a Judeo-Christian mystic, a traditional Pueblo Indian, or a Zen Buddhist.

When Peter Berg explains what is tourist and what is real, he says that being bioregional means "feeling continuous with the natural world around you." It means "not only identifying with the long-term interests of a place, but also seeing that what is out there is not 'other,' it is 'self.'"

"All of a sudden, when people say 'watershed,' they lower their voice a little. They know that a watershed is bigger than us. It contains us." Peter spreads his arms. "They say the words 'natural succession' and fully realize what an extraordinary idea it is. These things are becoming sacred to people. Why? You don't have to know why intellectually. It's where your allegiance lies. It's your home."

"We get struck all the time," Judy Goldhaft says. "We get awestruck. We get wonderstruck. I feel that connection as much as I can, to place, to the planet, to the power and the beauty and the wonder of the planet!"

Peter Berg once posed this question:

"Can growing your own little garden actually deal with the problem of destructive and poisonous agribusiness?"

His answer is pure bioregionalism.

Yes.

Is he overwhelmed by the gap between the world today and his vision of what it could be?

No.

Bioregionalism is not utopian. But it *is* optimistic. That may come from a hand-ons, get-your-hands-dirty, human-hands, Lizard-hands approach. "It's a proactive endeavor that doesn't smell futile from the beginning," says Peter. "It's not a place for martyrs."

It starts with the here and now.

Peter and Judy are urban. They live in a city and note, without judgment, that 75 percent of North Americans do too. Most of these people believe that water "comes from a faucet" and "food from the store." So, for the last five years, the Planet Drum Foundation has concentrated on helping cities think bioregionally. Their book, *A Green City Program,* addresses issues such as graywater, renewable energy, recycling, wildland corridors, and mass transportation.

"Urban people have to become urban pioneers," Peter says. "Take a bath, get a bucket, flush the toilet with your bathwater. You've just reduced 75 percent of pure water consumption!"

The profile of an urban pioneer might include riding a bicycle to work, growing peas in the backyard, recycling household wastes, using solar and wind energy systems, restoring wildlife habitat, and being active in neighborhood councils.

It starts with food.

"I look around at the Shasta bioregion, where I live," Peter says, "and I see that walnuts and almond trees and alfalfa probably aren't too far off from native bunchgrass and oaks. If there were deer eating the bunchgrass, it's not too far off from cows eating alfalfa. If there were indigenous people eating acorns, it's not too far off from an almond farm. The way we do it may have to change, the monoculture, the numbers, the way we use water. Bioregionalism is a cultural and social idea. I don't think people here have even *tried* sustainable agriculture. It hasn't been a consideration! We don't know that it can't be done."

It includes jobs.

"Reinhabitation begins with an act of faith. Then you find ways to support yourself." Peter Berg has two children, and he thinks seriously about how rural kids, city kids, bioregional kids, can make a living. He sees "thousands of job opportunities" in education, restoration, natural resource management, social and political activism—even ecotourism.

It means social responsibility.

"There are people out there who want to disinhabit you, to make you inauthentic. Gushing water fountains in Phoenix, big green golf courses, big green lawns in the desert! These are ways of disinhabiting people from the place where they live. It's criminal fraud. . . . The old western attitude of 'I can do anything I want on my land' has got to go. This is antisocial on a big order. If a biker were doing this, he'd be put in jail."

"The punitive approach," Peter adds, "isn't working. These people need to be encouraged to fit into a larger idea of community."

Judy Goldhaft has seen it happen.

In northern California, tens of thousands of king salmon used to head for the mouth of the Mattole River each year. By 1970, logging, overgrazing, and poorly built roads had caused so much silting that the salmon were nearly gone. A coalition of residents and resource managers formed the Mattole Watershed Salmon Support Group, a name that Judy says is "truly bioregional." The group captured fish as they returned to spawn and incubated the eggs until the fry emerged, thus keeping them from being buried in silt. At first, the restoration was opposed by local commodity interests. But gradually, with bioregional encouragement, local commodity interests turned into people who realized that they, too, wanted king salmon in the river.

Now the project has expanded to include erosion control and public education. The goal is for native residents (loggers, ranchers, grocery-store clerks, retirees, "leftovers from the hippie age") to manage and benefit from all local logging, grazing, and road work.

Culturally, Mattole schoolchildren paint murals about the spawning cycle. The town doctor has written a series of cabaret songs that celebrate fish. And there are women here who have learned to dance—to dance like salmon. This is a story of people living in place. This is the hope of a restored river, silver and sinuous, a young girl fishing from the shore.

Peter Berg stands before an audience. He talks about twelve pairs of mating peregrine falcons, recently released from Point Reyes. One day, two of these birds appeared on the roof of a downtown building in San Francisco. Peter is doing a gentle piece of ecocomedy. He digresses to mock the purpose of insurance companies. This particular high rise, chosen by the falcons, is called the Mutual Benefit Life Building.

"Straaange name," Peter drawls. "So these falcons, now, are hovering ten stories above the people below and *feeding on pigeons.* Here's a secretary doing her job or a chief executive describing some new bottom-line deal and they suddenly stop and say, '*What the hell was that!*' And outside the window . . . a puff of feathers explodes."

Peter imitates the sound of an exploding pigeon, *squaaaawk,* a sound of victory and surprise. The audience giggles—a bit hesitantly. "Falcons go at two hundred miles an hour," Peter tells them. "The fastest animal on earth! Those tall buildings are like canyons to them. They like the steep walls. They've got room to descend and pick up speed. . . . I think this is wonderful. The peregrine falcon, a longtime endangered species because of DDT, is *now reinhabiting the San Francisco Bay Area.*

"There's one more part of this story, the amazing part." Peter Berg leans over, confidentially. "They nest on the Bay Bridge." His audience chuckles. "They nest on the Bay Bridge," Peter pauses, "*and they commute, everyday, to the Mutual Benefit Life Building!*"

People laugh happily now. They like that idea. They like that connection.

Across town, on a different night, Judy Goldhaft performs "Water Web," a dance/narrative that is half movement and half poem. Her arms lift and elongate, circle and weave. Her body turns and tightens and tries to flow upward. She is dancing water even as she is talking about it. She lists, melodiously, our human names for this force: "Agua, aqua, atl, ab, uru, wasser, woda, waha, wai, ner, nis, pani, itzia, vellam, vatten, vand, vada, voda, viz, vesi, su, shui, mizu, maji, moyam, Ma . . . MA . . . MA."

She gives straight information: "Atmospheric water is replenished every twelve days."

She gives straight information that seems more dream than fact: "Running water slows itself by flowing in rhythmic loops."

She instructs: "The Code of Hammurabi, an influential early set of community laws, is almost entirely about water rights. Who owns the water."

"Who owns the Amazon," Judy insists, "the Ganges, the Mississippi? Who owns the Nile, the Zambezi, the Rhine? Who owns the Yangtze and the Volga?"

I think, of course, of the Mimbres River, water that I "bought" when I bought an irrigation right. My water amounts to 2.7 acre feet a year, enough water to spill out grandly onto the land. I can do this for half an hour every eleven days. If I do not irrigate for three years in a row—if I choose, for example, to leave the water in the river for a deer to drink or a fish to swim in—I will forfeit my right to irrigate at all. Use it or lose it, says our western Code of Hammurabi.

Judy's voice is deliberately like a stream, with perfect enunciation.

"Cleopatra bathed in our bathwater," she says.

"In the future"—she moves gracefully—"the limit of human population on earth will be determined by the availability of uncontaminated water. We have a responsibility toward all the water we pass through, toward all the water that passes through us."

She ends with a gesture that is quite beautiful. Like all human gestures, it is 70 percent water.

"I'd rather walk through a fire than walk away from one."
—*Madonna*

*"To put it in religious terms, the spiritual history of the world
is not over, and revelations as great as or greater than those
given to us in the past may yet be in store. One symptom of
the coming changes is the vigorous religious syncretism now
taking place in many parts of the world. . . . I know a Jungian
Catholic polytheist, an Iranian Sufi Hinduist Zorastrian, an
English Beshara Sufi Anglican pantheist, several Huichol
Zen humanist nature worshippers, and a Catholic Baha'i
transcendental meditator. This new breed of syncretists are not
kooks but people with a good sense of humor about their beliefs
and a sound understanding of science."*
—*Frederick Turner*

Of all domesticated animals, goats are probably the most interesting. Pigs may be smarter, but pigs have short legs and run too low
to the ground; they seem too much, too obviously, bred for meat.
Goats tend to be lean and feisty and independent. Their triangular
heads remind us of deer. Their eyes, set wide apart, focus intently.
They are looking for predators. They are looking for fun. Someone
is behind those eyes.

I have raised goats and, like other "nouveau country," I was re-
lieved when we sold our last pair. Simply put, goats can be too much
of a good thing. Gallon jars of milk dominate the refrigerator. Bags
of goat cheese hang from every corner. Goats must be milked twice
a day, and they must be bred for them to produce more milk. Expo-

nentially, they multiply. Two goats, quickly, become six. I was glad to put down this burden of abundance. At the same time, I miss goats. I miss their very presence, in the way that people miss the *geist* of a cat or dog in the house.

Jim Corbett—goatherd, prophet, and public-lands rancher—is from Wyoming. At the age of nine, he toyed with the idea of becoming a preacher. "You'll get over it," his mother said. He ended up with a degree in philosophy from Harvard. He married, had three children, and painfully divorced. He cowboyed and ranched in Arizona. Later he discovered that he was a Quaker—not a Christian, but a man who found "something like love that doesn't split, the way love does, into loving and being loved." He worked as a sheepherder, antiwar organizer, college librarian, teacher, Forest Service employee, park ranger, and horse trader. He remarried, a woman he describes as "Sancha to my Quixote, Quixote to my Sancho." He begins his book, *Goatwalking: A Guide to Wildland Living and a Quest for the Peaceable Kingdom,* with this central idea: "Two milk goats can provide all the nutrients a human being needs with the exception of vitamin C and a few common trace elements. Learn the relevant details about range-goat husbandry and something about edible plants, and with a couple of milk goats you can feed yourself in most wildlands, even in deserts."

Jim is serious. In the Sonoran Desert, where he lives, goats can eat various parts of prickly pear, mesquite, cholla, creosote, palo verde, ironwood, rabbitbrush, manzanita, hackberry, tumbleweed, snakeweed, and catclaw acacia. These tough and thorny plants are made of water, dirt, and sky. Goats turn them into food. The goatwalker takes the gift, moving the herd often so as not to damage the land from which the gift comes. This is nomadic pastoralism. It is, for Jim Corbett, a form of Quixotic errantry—a sallying forth beyond the limits of what most Americans know. The goatwalker fits "into an ecological niche rather than a social hierarchy." The goatwalker, for however brief a time, is no longer a member of industrial civilization and is no longer forced to "make war on life." The goatwalker has gone feral. Wandering, "useless," Bodhisattva-inspired, the goatwalker is at home in a world defined sternly by eight inches of annual rainfall.

As a teacher, Jim was once asked what he would do to educate teenagers. Naturally he suggested goatwalking. Ontogeny repeats phylogeny: the developmental history of the amphibious fetus mimics the developmental history of our species. Jim Corbett believes that "cultural ontogeny *must* also repeat cultural phylogeny." To know where we are, we must know where we came from.

"Everyone should learn how to feed himself or herself," Jim says amiably. "Everyone should live for a time as a member of a tribal band. Goatwalking is a practical way to do this. Hunting and gathering requires a lot of skill and has too great an impact on the land. Gardening and subsistence agriculture need time and take specific conditions. But people can learn to goatwalk fairly easily."

Goatwalking is a word, a rather new word, laden with meaning.

In the last half of the 1970s, Jim and his wife Pat were part of a goat-milking cooperative called *Los Cabreros Andantes* or "the goatherds errant." For three years, they visited and lived with a community of seminomadic goatherds in the Mexican state of Baja California Sur. *Los Cabreros Andantes* gathered Nubian buck kids from the United States and bred them in the mountains of South Baja. The Nubians helped increase the herds' milk production. The Mexican herders taught the Americans about living in place in the desert.

Jim and Pat were pursuing a land-based livelihood—a biocentric ethic and a bioregional partnership. In "The Goat Cheese Economy of the South Baja Sierras," published in *The Dairy Goat Journal* in 1979, Jim proposed an "economic development that is an aspect of community growth rather than political subjugation or technocratic alienation."

What he says next is confusing, unless you know his terms.

A cimarron is a slave or domesticated animal that goes free. In the Bible, Abraham and Moses and the Hebrews went cimarron. Nomadic pastoralists everywhere identify with this idea. To go cimarron today is to free oneself from technocracy, hierarchy, and possession. Cimarrons do not possess the earth; they accept its gifts.

Zionism, according to Jim Corbett, is the process of becoming a holy people who establish themselves in a specific land and "hallow the earth" through covenants with the land and each other.

"I have no plans or techniques to suggest," Jim concluded his article in *The Dairy Goat Journal,* "but active friendship with those who are at home on the land—meeting, sharing, and learning—would be a beginning for most gringos. Land redemption within the United States—a kind of wildland Zionism replacing degenerative commercial uses with cimarron communities at home and at peace with untamed life—might come next."

These are ancient, meaning-laden words that Jim Corbett did not use until he was in his late forties. He had goatwalked as a Taoist, a Buddhist, and a philosopher. He had goatwalked as a literary, educational, and practical exercise. He viewed the Bible "as something we have to get over."

"Yet I couldn't avoid seeing that the way had already been blazed," he would write later. "Goatwalking reenacts the history of the prophetic faith. Contrary to my preconceptions and aversions, goatwalking is biblical."

Everything is connected.

Goatwalking is the ability to go cimarron, to walk away from one's masters. Quakers also believe that it is sometimes necessary to walk away from the demands of the government or an unjust law. In 1981, Jim and Pat were living in Tucson, at the end of a dirt road, with a corral for Pat's mule, a pen for the goats, a chicken coop, a garden, and a tumble of cats, dogs, and geese. One night, at supper, a friend told them about a hitchhiker he had picked up that day, a frightened Salvadoran later arrested at a Border Patrol roadblock. Jim

Corbett remembered thirteen other Salvadorans who had died the previous summer in Organ Pipe National Monument; like many Central American refugees, they were from the city, in a strange land, under a hot sun. Jim and Pat asked their friend about El Salvador. It was a horror story that most Americans, to this day, do not fully understand. The next morning, Jim woke up with the conviction that he had to find this hitchhiker.

In the coming weeks, Jim Corbett immersed himself in the reality of Salvadoran refugees and immigration law. He did, finally, meet the man he was looking for, only to see him quickly deported. In the early 1980s, thousands of people were fleeing the civil war and death squads of Central America. Very few were granted asylum in the United States. They came anyway, secretly, across the searing Sonoran and Chihuahuan deserts. What choice did they have? Jim Corbett knew how to survive in these deserts. He knew the mountains of southern Arizona particularly well from his days managing cattle on the Flying H ranch. He spoke Spanish. He had been up and down the border. He was uniquely suited to help.

By 1984, a coalition of churches and synagogues throughout the United States had openly declared their intent to shield refugees from unjust deportation. With some reverence, this was known as Sanctuary. Jim Corbett had abandoned his more comfortable pursuit of a land ethic in order to fill an immediate need. He traveled across Mexico, networking, counseling, writing, and talking. He guided desperate men, women, and children into canyon bottoms, across dry washes, over hot rock, through fields of cactus, to the border fence. He worked often with priests. At times, he even allowed prison and border officials to believe that he was one. He became known as a *cuaquero muy catolico*—a very Catholic Quaker.

His own idiosyncratic phrasing served as policy for the Tucson Ecumenical Council's Task Force on Central America: "The covenant to become a people that hallows the earth has always entailed that the beneficiaries of oppression relinquish their allegiance to wealth, privilege, and domination, taking their stand with the poor and persecuted. . . . "

In 1985, a dozen Sanctuary leaders and activists—including Nena MacDonald, who would later move to the Gila Valley to help form the conservation group Friends of the Gila River—were indicted for conspiring to violate U.S. immigration law. Jim and Nena and one other were acquitted, the rest put on probation. By now, Jim's high profile had made him relatively useless as a border guide. Thankfully, he and Pat returned to their goats.

Everything is connected: land and people and ecology and justice and goats and cowboys.

Sanctuary was a covenant "to treat no one as violable, an enemy, or an alien." Jim had learned a lot about rules and regulations and the court system. But none of that mattered to him as much as the covenant of Sanctuary that people made in their hearts and daily lives. So, too, with the land.

"Extending the morality of basic rights to include land," Jim says, "has nothing to do, initially, with public rather than private ownership or with passing new statutes. It has to do with a community practice that weaves the land's rights into the social fabric. This approach is contrary to the way environmental activism is usually done. Environmentalists generally urge intervention by the state as a cure-all for the greed and destruction done by property owners. This is fundamentally at odds with covenanting."

In 1988, Jim and Pat and some of their goatherding friends formed the Saguaro-Juniper Association. They bought more than one hundred acres of private property near the San Pedro River and a grazing lease for six square miles of state-owned hills, mountains, mesas, and canyons. A smaller group called *El Potrero* also purchased some adjacent irrigated farmland. Both groups made a covenant with these hills. They planned to run some goats, some cows, some burros perhaps. They got involved, inevitably and immediately, in the new range war between ranchers and environmentalists.

Once again the division seemed so clear to so many people, between alien and citizen, between friend and enemy.

It is mid-August and we sit outside, by the trailer. The air darkens. Monsoon clouds roil over the desert mountains, blocking out the sun and filling the sky with fierce purpose. Jim's hands and feet are arthritic, painfully twisted. Awkwardly, he holds his coffee cup.

Most of the time now, he and Pat live in this small trailer on *El Potrero*'s deeded, irrigated land. The goat pens are once again nearby. There is another garden patch and a gabble of chickens. At the river bottom, the elevation starts at 3,000 feet and climbs in a series of gravelly hills to 4,500. Jim knows the grasses best: black grama, sideoats grama, hairy grama, sprucetop grama, and various blue stems. Junipers and oaks grow in the shade of the higher mountain tops. Saguaros dominate hot, south-facing slopes. The association has a state permit to graze here twenty-nine head of livestock yearlong. They plan to do a lot of monitoring, particularly of saguaro regeneration. Pat Corbett studied range management and once worked for the BLM; Jim did range analysis back in the 1950s; a number of people in the Saguaro-Juniper Association are scientists. This is a community effort.

"If I am going to be at home in the Sonoran Desert," Jim says, "genuinely at home where the land is supporting me, then grazing is the only option. Mining isn't. Nor is a salaried job in Tucson where I'm like someone on the moon with a life support system. No, if I'm to be at home here—and I don't have any other home— then I have to look at specific ways and places where my relationship with the land can be harmonious."

"Those of us who want to graze," he adds, "have the burden of proof."

He does not expect to make money ranching. He and others in the association will get food, a place to live, a place to visit, and a way to answer some questions about range management. This is research combined with subsistence living. This is, unsurprisingly, religion and metaphor.

To some degree, Jim is echoing the beliefs of many Native Americans in the Southwest. The Navajos, in particular, have integrated sheepherding into their cultural and spiritual heritage. Livestock comes "dressed in rain," and the herding of livestock is part of a sacred way of life.

Jim Corbett talks about the sabbath.

When Moses climbed Mount Nebo to die, he looked down at his people, "settled, growing fat, surrounded by owner worship." How could they keep to their God? How could they keep to their covenant?

The Lord told them how. Each seventh day, they should cease to labor. Each seventh week of harvest, they should feast and remember that they were a cimarron people. Each seventh month, they should leave their homes and live in brush shelters as they had done in the desert. Each seventh year, they should stop living by agriculture.

"The sabbath is a time," Jim says, "to quit grabbing at the world, to rest, and to rejoice in the Creation's goodness." It is a time of wilderness and cimarron remembrance. Jim Corbett does this through goatwalking. He does it every Friday night when he recites the Shema and other passages from the Jewish prayer book. He does it through the Saguaro-Juniper Association. For its members, this land by the San Pedro River is meant to serve as a sabbatical *place*, rather than a sabbatical time, a place where humans can live out the covenant. It is such a place precisely because it has not been "protected" in the sense of being set apart from humans. It is a place where goats and cows eat plants and turn them into food.

"A land ethic is not a preserve mentality," Jim says. "You are a co-member of the community, a co-creator. You're not some alien visiting another planet. A land ethic is not about living off the industrial and technological resources of a city and going out, once in a while, to appreciate the scenery.

"If creation is incomplete, as it is, then it's because we are still creating ourselves. Whether we like it or not, the biblical passages about governance happen to be the fact. We are reflective. We make decisions and choices in a way that other creatures do not. We have a fundamental choice now between possessing the earth and trying to enter into a hallowing process. We are called upon to be co-creators. It's the alternative to being possessors.

"As a co-creator, you never know everything that's going on. You are working within a system rather than being outside and manipulating it. That sense of being *outside* is the management mode. But as a co-creator, you never know if you've got it right conclusively. You don't have a god's omnipresent eye."

We are inside the circle.

We are part of nature and dependent on nature.

"If you look at society as an ecosystem," Jim says, "then you see that it's not a matter of getting it organized right with the right guy in charge. This is how technocrats think, that society is an object they can manipulate. Instead, they are really acting within the ecosystem."

Jim Corbett knows that one way to manipulate society is to polarize issues. He quotes from Saul Alinsky's *Rules for Radicals,* a book that helped develop our modern style of political organization. Alinsky wrote, "Men will act when they are convinced that their cause is 100 percent on the side of the angels and that the opposition are 100 percent on the side of the devil." In his Rule Thirteen, the organizer thundered, "Pick the target, freeze it, personalize it, and polarize it."

"In the Saul Alinsky style, that's how you mobilize a group," Jim says. "That's how you generate action. Today, the environmental movement has all sorts of different agendas pulling people different ways. Global warming, acid rain, diminishing rain forests. Now suddenly the cow is being used as a common enemy! The cow has become the uniting symbol of what needs to go. I thought the conflict had plateaued, but it hasn't. There is a constantly growing intensity among people without a corresponding understanding of what this is all about. But there is also a growing alliance among informed conservationists and informed ranchers. It's a race as to who is going to get there first."

For Jim Corbett, the first thing is to get those people who seem most opposed to sit down together. "There are all sorts of creative possibilities which they can't even *see* when they are only fighting each other," he says. "We really live in symbiosis. We are mutually supportive parts of something larger."

In southeastern Arizona, Jim has become active in the self-named Malpais Group. This handful of men and women believe deeply in the importance of the traditional ranching lifestyle. That's nothing new; it's the premise of every cattle growers' convention. But the Malpais Group has also invited "opponents" such as Dave Foreman and Lynn Jacobs to their meetings. They've spoken at the bioregional Sonoran People's Summit. They support the reintroduction of the Mexican wolf. They are against indiscriminate predator control. They are trying to listen.

"This war may mean the end for us," one Malpais rancher told me. "But if we somehow survive, and if all this makes ranchers look at what they are doing—if we get some good changes—then maybe it's worth it."

Jim Corbett writes: "Just as heedlessly as industrial civilization displaces untamed biotic communities, it is burning its bridges with livelihoods that are rooted in humanity's pre-industrial relations with the land. Keeping our options open by preserving these livelihoods is a matter of ecological wisdom, not just an exercise in nostalgia. Particularly in the case of ranching in the West's arid lands, we need greater diversity, not eradication."

He writes: "Farming might replace ranching economically, but it can't substitute culturally. Livelihoods based on human adaptation to the land (in contrast to adaptations such as farming that adapt the

land to us) are irreplaceable microcosms in which to initiate humanity's ecological task, to discover how to live at peace with the rest of
life on earth. . . . Commercial ranching is not really subsistence living. But it could be an approximation. It doesn't require ripping out
existing biotic communities and putting in some cultigen or completely foreign landscape."

He writes: "I agree with Aldo Leopold that a land ethic (in which
human beings are partners rather than conquerors of the biotic
community) has become 'an evolutionary possibility and an ecological necessity.' It is, however, a possibility only where human beings
are still at home on the land. How to fit in responsibly (as supportive
members of an untamed biotic community) is a meaningful question
only for those who live by fitting in somehow."

Ranching, in this view, becomes a sabbatical occupation—another
way for humans to remember the covenant.

On this August afternoon, in the glory of this rainy season, Jim
Corbett sits and drinks coffee. He is a gnarly weathered man who
resembles, in his own mind, "Don Quixote with glasses." The sky
darkens, darkens, darkens, and finally lets loose. We rush to the trailer.
Inside, we perch on the couch and try to talk above the noise of rain
on tin. Lightning illuminates the air between us with flashes that are
too bright and too powerful. Thunder cracks like a gunshot in the
bedroom. It is shooting up the goat's pen, exploding on the doorstep,
crashing against the closed window. The thinnest layers of metal and
glass separate us from the storm. But, we know, really, that we are not
separate. We are vulnerable. We are involved. Later, as I drive the dirt
road back to the town of Benson and Interstate 10, I will drive on
mirrored sheets of water. I will splash home and pause seriously before each arroyo. They are running strong.

All that is in the future.

Now we are talking about ranching.

Jim Corbett's kind of ranching, co-creation, requires the very specific knowledge that Peter Berg and Allan Savory and Connie Hat-

field insist on. Are the goats imitating the use patterns of local deer? If so, are they displacing deer or adding to a too-large population? What equine would best browse this invasive species? What is the natural succession of plants in this field? What is the role of fire in this canyon? Why are saguaros regenerating on that slope and not on this one? Everything is connected—plants, animals, insects, disease, fire, topography, weather—from the spiral crab nebula to the genes of the crayfish.

Obviously, Jim Corbett is not your average rancher. Instead, he is living proof that a very very good rancher can out-environmental the environmentalist, hands down.

The Saguaro-Juniper Covenant includes this bill of rights:

1. The land has a right to be free of human activity that accelerates erosion.

2. Native plants and animals on the land have a right to life with a minimum of human disturbance.

3. The land has the right to evolve its own character from its own elements without scarring from construction or the importation of foreign objects dominating the scene.

4. The land has a preeminent right to the preservation of its unique or rare constituents and features.

5. The land, its waters, rocks, and minerals, its plants and animals, and their fruits and harvest have a right never to be rented, sold, extracted, or exported as mere commodities.

Lightning blazes in the little trailer. God is drumming on the roof.

"Ranching is not a business like any other," Jim says. "It's not going to pay off the mortgage and make a living and be a return on an investment in the same way as if you started a pizza parlor. The component difference between what is fully commercial and what isn't has to be made up through love of the land. There's no business reason to ranch if you don't have that active love.

"You can't get this love, this intimacy, easily or quickly. You have to be there, nurtured by the land, to develop that real, cimarron wis-

dom. That's why it's so important to nurture ranchers who are conservationists. If we lose that wisdom, it can't be created very readily.

"There's been a lot of damage done by ranchers. Part of that was
ignorance. Part was greed and laziness. Part was the nature of industrial civilization, the need to press the land to pay off a mortgage or
to produce more and more and more.

"Still," Jim says, "there are good reasons to try and integrate
ranching with the interests of the larger biotic community."

The rain eases slightly. We no longer have to shout.

Jim Corbett is not opposed to pristine, ungrazed wilderness areas.
He'd be "very reluctant to take grazing into places where it has been
withdrawn." He believes that Allan Savory provides a "good working
conceptual tool," although he quibbles with Savory's philosophy and
biology. He thinks that the current range war is more volatile and
dangerous than any of his activities in Sanctuary. He admits that most
of the violence comes from ranchers.

Instead of raising the grazing fee on public lands, he has an alternative scheme. It involves recognizing the private property value attached to the federal grazing permit, allowing ranchers to sell back
their AUMs to the government just as they sell them to each other,
and then adjusting the fees to reflect the real market value established by that sales price. In many cases, money that ranchers now
are paying to a bank would go instead to a federal range program.
Ranchers themselves would no longer be tempted to overstock simply because the grazing fee was cheap.

"Below-market fees for anything creates excessive demands and
entrenched 'underground' markets that resist reform," Jim says. "The
trick is in making the shift in a way that lets ranchers keep their de
facto equities, while shifting the private market in permits over to
the fees side of the balance."

About some aspects of deep ecology and the despair that some
environmentalists feel, Jim Corbett is wary.

"I can't go along with the idea that humanity just needs to slowly fade out of the picture—or ideally, commit suicide—and everything will be fine," he says. "There's an altruistic passivity there, a kind of self-loathing. I don't think any ecological concept that preaches disempowerment will ever get anywhere."

Jim quotes Spinoza, his favorite philosopher. "We are all modes in the Body of Being."

There is a sudden and very loud silence. Storms come and go this fast in the desert.

"Nothing," Jim says sweetly, "is outside the Body of Being."

We *are* syncretic. We pick and choose.

Like Bernice Naranjo, I have my own view, my own image.

An essay on nature by John Fowles describes the mythical "man in the trees" who in "all his manifestations, as dryad, as stag-headed Herne, as outlaw" possesses somehow the power and elusiveness of the trees. "I am certain," Fowles wrote, "that the attraction of the myth is so profound and universal because it is constantly 'played' inside every individual consciousness. This notion of the green man . . ."

Stop.

Let's call her the green woman.

Let's call her the green woman, an elusive dryad hidden in our hardened modern selves. A powerful green force. A generous spirit.

Let's call her the green woman, and let's call her out. Let's call her out in every cowboy and rancher, Christian and non-Christian, Navajo and Nez Perce, Anglo and Hispanic and black, ecologist and environmentalist, in the city and in the country, in homosexuals and heterosexuals, in teachers and writers and farmers and mothers and fathers and grocery-store clerks, in the range con and in the district ranger, in the feed-store owner and the health-food buyer, in all of us who live here and make this our home. Let's call her out.

Let's see what she has to say about the West.

5. EPILOGUE

Pessimism comes from the repression of creativity.
—*Otto Rank*

SITTING ON the fence can be an uncomfortable position. For some things, it's a good place to get a view. Eventually you have to jump off and pitch camp.

I believe that within the next twenty years there will be less grazing on the public land. I believe there should be less grazing.

A number of areas are being degraded by the presence of cattle. Changing management might solve the problem. More often, a total rest from grazing is necessary. Land health is the bottom line. Sustainability is our touchstone. Ecology is the only true lens.

In some places, especially near cities, ranching will decline simply because public land has become more valuable in terms of recreation and aesthetics. By and large, people in Denver want to see elk, not heifers. They want wildlife and the smell of wilderness. This is a valid cultural and economic shift. I believe that Jim Corbett is right: as a society, we must preserve our ranching traditions as a way of preserving our connections to the land. But we do not need to graze 70 percent of the West to do this. More obviously, we cannot all become ranchers. Most of us will continue to live in urban areas. Most of us can only visit the western landscape, our life support systems carefully centralized. How, then, can we become better visitors? How can we find new ways of being at home on the earth?

I believe that people like Steve Johnson, Judy Goldhaft, Peter Berg, Lori Fish, Jim Corbett, Doc and Connie Hatfield, Denzel and Nancy Ferguson, Steve and Nena MacDonald, Tito and Bernice Naranjo, Guy Connolly, Dan Moore, Susan Larson, Carol Martingale, Don Oman, Allan Savory, and Pamela Brown are each, separately, trying to answer these questions.

I do not believe that the economics of ranching is as important as the ecology of ranching. A low grazing fee may or may not be a significant subsidy. But raising that fee will not necessarily—on its own—be good for the land. There must also be incentives for ranchers to become good stewards, as well as ways to retire degraded allotments. With any increase in operating costs, some ranchers will squeeze the land harder to make it pay in the short term. Ranches that do go bankrupt will simply revert to the bank and new owners. As long as grazing is mandated by Forest Service and BLM regulations, only the players will change, not the game.

I do not believe in "Cattle-free by 2003." Some public land is compatible with ranching. Some land is even better maintained as a ranch rather than being checkerboarded with fences, condos, and vacation homes.

We must remember Allan Savory's three-part goal. We must know what we want.

Does any serious rancher not want land health? Does any serious rancher not want sustainability? Does any serious environmentalist not recognize the need for people to be at home on the land? Who is the environmentalist's ally against the growing air pollution of our forests and range? Against toxic wastes in the water? Against irresponsible overdevelopment? Who is the rancher's ally?

We must know what we want and see what we have in common.

There is no blanket solution. Northern New Mexico is not southern Montana. We must decide these things place by place. With some trepidation, I believe that the best people to make these decisions are those who have chosen to live in or near that place. This includes people in urban areas like Phoenix or Albuquerque. Forest Service and BLM resource managers must and can help. Integrated resource management teams and interdisciplinary teams are a good start. If they are a sham now, make them real. If they are unwieldy and slow, don't be surprised. Bringing people together is a slow process. Building community is like building topsoil.

If a goal is clear and honest, it can provide its own light.

If the goal is to have regional empowerment and decision making, based on land health and sustainability, then we will find ways to encourage that. Those in the middle can begin to mediate. The career ladder of government agencies can allow for men and women who want to root rather than climb. Local groups can help collect field data. Girl Scouts can plant willows. Bird-watchers can count birds. Absentee and corporate permittees can be required to participate or to accept that their power is greatly diminished by distance. The Forest Service might begin to host potlucks; the BLM will have a dance.

Obviously, a lot of people won't come.

Does it work? Is it honorable?

I'm not saying that these are easy questions. I'm not saying that we will all have the same answers.

I believe that Americans should eat less meat and pay more for the meat we do eat.

I do not believe we should import beef or support the destruction of any ecosystem anywhere.

I believe we should encourage the gray wolf to recolonize naturally. I believe we should reintroduce the Mexican wolf.

I believe in wilderness and large expanses of wildlife habitat because wilderness and wildlife have an intrinsic right to exist. Moreover, we need them. Wilderness proponents ask for so little: a small percentage of the contiguous United States, the barest fraction of this planet, tiny slivers of land. This is an important compromise between humanity and the rest of the earth.

I believe that cattle should be slowly and honorably phased out of most wilderness areas, wildlife refuges, and national monuments.

I believe the Animal Damage Control program must wrest itself from the control of livestock growers. No one group should dominate a federal agency. ADC needs to talk and listen to more environmentalists. ADC should not operate on the public lands. At the same time, environmentalists must move beyond their comfort zone. Wildlife management, like wilderness preservation, is an oxymoron we all have to live with.

I believe we should retire grazing allotments for ecological reasons.

I believe in compensation for ranchers.

I believe that we need the cowboy. We need every root and roothair.

I believe in a biodiversity of myth.

Remembrance is an acknowledgment of the past, of all that was good and all that was bad.

Repentance is a transformation lured by the vision of what the future could be.

SELECTED BIBLIOGRAPHY
AND NOTES

CHAPTER ONE

Pages 1–13

The quote from Frederick Turner can be found in *Waning of the West* (St. Martin's Press, 1989), by Stan Steiner. The quote by Jay McDaniel is from his essay "Christianity and the Need for New Vision," in *Religion and Environmental Crisis* (University of Georgia Press, 1986) edited by Eugene C. Hargrove.

The quote concerning early investments in cattle can be found in *The Day of the Cattleman* (University of Chicago Press, 1929), by Ernest Staples Osgood. The quote from the former head of the Grazing Section of the early Forest Service comes from *United States Forest Service Grazing and Rangelands: A History* (Texas A&M University Press, 1985), by William Rowley. Other historical sources are *Natural Resources for the 21st Century* (Island Press, 1990), edited by R. Neil Sampson and Dwight Hair; *Waste of the West* (Jacobs, 1991), by Lynn Jacobs; and *Land and Resource Planning in the National Forests* (Island Press, 1987), by Charles F. Wilkinson and Michael Anderson. *A Legacy of Change* (University of Arizona Press, 1991), by Conrad Joseph Bahre, also discusses the role of fire and drought in the West.

Statistics on the health of our rangeland come from the 1988 GAO report *Rangeland Management: More Emphasis Needed on Declining and Overstocked Grazing Allotments*; the 1988 GAO report *Public Rangelands: Some Riparian Areas Restored But Widespread Improvement Will Be Slow*; and *Our Ailing Public Rangelands,* a report by the National Wildlife Federation and the Natural

Resources Defense Council. Information from the 1992 report to the United Nations Conference on Environment and Development was first published in *Worldwatch Paper 103, Taking Stock: Animal Farming and the Environment* (Worldwatch, 1991), by Alan B. Durning and Holly B. Brough. Information concerning riparian conditions also can be found in Ed Chaney's *Livestock Grazing on Western Riparian Areas* (Eagle, Idaho: Northwest Resource Information Center) and the 1988 GAO report *Public Rangelands: Some Riparian Areas Restored But Widespread Improvement Will Be Slow.* In personal correspondence, Harold Dregne, professor of soil science at Texas Tech University, provided me with additional statistics on the desertification of North America.

The publication *Worldwatch Paper 103* provides a good summary of the livestock industry in global terms.

The amount that a cow drinks daily was provided by the Forest Service.

Information on the use of water in the West can be found in many sources, including *Overtapped Oasis: Reform or Revolution for Western Waters* (Island Press, 1990), by Marc Reisner and Sarah Bates; Lynn Jacobs's *Waste of the West*; and *Beyond Beef: The Rise and Fall of the Cattle Culture* (Dutton, 1992), by Jeremy Rifkin.

How much beef public-lands ranchers produce can be found in the 1992 *Grazing Fee Review and Evaluation Update of the 1986 Final Report,* produced jointly by the Department of Agriculture and the Department of the Interior. I also consulted the 1992 report *The Importance of Public Lands to Livestock Production in the United States,* by the Range Improvement Task Force at New Mexico State University.

Statistics on how much federal land is grazed can be found in the 1992 *Grazing Fee Review and Evaluation Update of the 1986 Final Report,* as can the current number of permittees.

The membership of environmental organizations is listed in the *Encyclopedia of Associations, 26th Edition, 1992.*

Statistics on the relationship of public-lands ranchers to other livestock producers comes from the 1992 *Grazing Fee Review and Evaluation Update.*

Allan Savory is discussed further in chapter two. His theories are best explained in his book *Holistic Resource Management* (Island Press, 1985). The range studies in the Chihuahuan Desert are cited by Dr. Jerry Holechek, a professor in the Department of Animal and Range Sciences at New Mexico State University.

The quote from Aldo Leopold is from his classic *Sand County Almanac.*

CHAPTER TWO

Pages 14–27/Denzel and Nancy Ferguson

The quote from William Kittredge is from *Owning It All* (Greywolf Press, 1987).

The material concerning Denzel and Nancy Ferguson comes from personal interviews and correspondence.

Statistics concerning the Malheur National Wildlife Refuge are taken from *Sacred Cows at the Public Trough* (Maverick Publications, 1983), by Denzel and Nancy Ferguson. The refuge also is specifically discussed in a 1989 GAO report, *National Wildlife Refuges: Continuing Problems with Incompatible Uses Call for Bold Action.*

Further material on the effects of cows on riparian areas can be found in Ed Chaney's *Livestock Grazing on Western Riparian Areas* (Eagle, Idaho: Northwest Resource Information Center) and the 1988 GAO report *Public Rangelands: Some Riparian Areas Restored But Widespread Improvement Will Be Slow.* The Camp Creek Exclosure is discussed in the latter. Harold Winegar, a retired biologist with the Oregon Department of Fish and Wildlife, also provided me with information concerning Camp Creek.

Nancy's statistics on how many ranchers graze how many cows came partially from a 1984 *Appraisal Report Estimating Fair Market Rental Value,* prepared by the Forest Service and the BLM, as well as from the 1992 *Grazing Fee Review and Evaluation Update of the 1986 Final Report,* produced jointly by the Department of Agriculture and the Department of the Interior. The 1991 GAO *Rangeland Management: BLM's Hot Desert Grazing Program Merits Reconsideration* confirms that ranching is not economical for many BLM operators. The figure concerning original permits to families is from Lynn Jacobs's *Waste of the West.*

Nancy's figures on sedimentation are found in her book *Sacred Cows at the Public Trough.*

Nancy's statistics concerning the grazing fee and the cost of the federal range program are confirmed in the 1992 *Grazing Fee Review and Evaluation Update of the 1986 Final Report.*

Pages 27–41/Steve and Nena MacDonald

The material concerning Steve and Nena MacDonald comes from interviews and personal correspondence.

There are a number of handbooks that help an environmentalist "adopt an allotment." One is *How Not to Be Cowed* (Natural Resources Defense Council and the Southern Utah Alliance for Wilderness, 1991).

More information on *Ganados del Valle* can be found in "The Workbook: Revitalizing Hispanic and Native American Communities," produced by the Southwest Research and Information Center in Albuquerque.

The statistic on native ecosystems in the Southwest comes from the 1988 Arizona State Parks Wetlands Priority Plan.

Pages 42–55/Don Oman

Material concerning Don Oman comes from interviews and personal correspondence.

Lynn Jacobs's *Waste of the West* is a good source for "an environmentalist's history" of grazing on public land. So is *Public Grazing Lands: Use and Misuse by Industry and Government* (Rutgers University Press, 1976), by William Voigt, Jr. Other histories include *United States Forest Service Grazing and Rangelands: A History* (Texas A&M University, 1985), by William Rowley, and *Land and Resource Planning in the National Forests* (Island Press, 1987), by Charles F. Wilkinson and Michael Anderson. *Storm Over Rangeland: Private Rights in Federal Lands* (Free Enterprise Press, 1989), by Wayne Hage discusses the concept of the "split estate" of our federal lands.

Statistics concerning the size and makeup of the Forest Service and BLM come from the Department of Agriculture and the Department of the Interior.

Don Oman's whistle-blower's complaint contain the worksheets he was given by the Forest Service, as well as other information about Oman's career in Twin Falls. The investigator's comments were taken directly from his report PS-899-0021.

A number of articles have appeared about Don Oman. These include those in the *High Country News,* May 7, 1990; *New York Times,* August 19, 1990; *Western Livestock Journal,* May 6, 1991; *Wilderness,* Spring 1991; *Audubon,* March, 1991; and *People* magazine, August 1991.

Pages 56–73/Doc and Connie Hatfield

The quote by John Erickson is from *Ranching Traditions* (Cross River Press, 1989), edited by Alan Axelrod. The quote by Doris Lessing is from her book *African Laughter* (HarperCollins, 1992).

Material concerning Doc and Connie Hatfield and Allan Savory comes from interviews and personal correspondence.

Allan Savory's theories are best described in his book *Holistic Resource Management* (Island Press, 1985).

The journal *Rangelands* contained the quoted article "Southern Africa's Experience with Intensive Short Duration Grazing," by Jon Skovlin, in its August 1987 issue.

The range studies suggesting the benefits of moderate to light grazing are cited by Dr. Jerry Holechek, a professor in the Department of Animal and Range Sciences at New Mexico State University.

The percentages of livestock on public land come from *The Importance of Public Lands to Livestock Production in the U.S.* by the New Mexico Range Improvement Task Force.

Carl and Jane Bock cite more studies concerning this subject in their paper *Effects of 22 Years' Livestock Exclusion in an Arizona Grassland* presented at a grazing symposium sponsored by the National Park Service in Flagstaff, Arizona. The Bocks are researchers at the Audubon Research Center and are associated with the Department of Biology, University of Colorado. This paper also compares the Audubon land to nearby ranches managed with HRM.

CHAPTER THREE

Pages 76–89/Steve Johnson

The quote by Aldo Leopold is from *Sand County Almanac.*

Some of the information about Dale Lee comes from *Life of the Greatest Guide: Hound Stories and Others of Dale Lee* (Blue River Graphics, 1979), by Robert McCurdy.

Historical information about ADC and predator control in the United States can be found in the 1990 GAO report *Wildlife Management: Effects of Animal Damage Control Programs on Predators,* and in *Predator Control and the Sheep Industry: The Role of Science in Policy Formation* (Regina Books, 1988), by Frederick H. Wagner.

Material concerning Steve Johnson, Guy Connolly, and Darryl Juve (Arizona state director of ADC) comes from interviews and personal correspondence.

There have been many articles on ADC. The *High Country News* spotlighted ADC in its January 28, 1991, story titled "A Federal Killing Machine Rolls On."

ADC's 1988 environmental impact statement gives a summary of its current practices and procedures.

The numbers of animals killed during fiscal year 1990 was obtained from the Animal Damage Control staff in Hyattsville, Maryland.

Information on funding and on the costs for ADC can be found in its EIS report and in the 1990 GAO report *Wildlife Management: Effects of Animal Damage Control Programs on Predators.* Guy Connolly also provided me with statistics on this subject.

More information on the desert tortoise can be found in the 1989 GAO report *California Desert: Planned Wildlife Protection and Enhancement Objectives Not Achieved.*

Steve Johnson is referring to the 1991 GAO report *Rangeland Management: BLM's Hot Desert Grazing Program Merits Reconsideration.*

Pages 90–101 / Guy Connolly

The quote by Harley Shaw comes from his book *Soul Among Lions: The Cougar as Peaceful Adversary* (Johnson Publishing Company, 1989).

Statistics on ADC's annual average kills come from its 1988 EIS report.

Information on funding and on the costs for ADC can be found in its EIS report and in the 1990 GAO report *Wildlife Management: Effects of Animal Damage Control Programs on Predators.* Guy Connolly also provided me with statistics on this subject.

Statistics on the ADC's annual average kills come from its 1988 EIS report.

The Wyoming sting operation was discussed in the *Sunday Denver Post*'s article "Feds: Ranchers Poisoning Eagles" on September 15, 1991, as well as in other newspapers and magazines.

Losses of sheep and goats to predators can be found in a 1991 report by the National Agricultural Statistics Service. Losses of calves and cows to predators are in a 1992 report by the National Agricultural Statistics Service.

Dr. John Grandy, vice president of the Humane Society of the United States, provided me with information concerning the secretary of agriculture's National Animal Damage Control Advisory Committee.

More information on wildlife in the United States can be found in the 1991 GAO report *Public Land Management: Attention to Wildlife Is Limited.*

Figures on the bald eagle can be found in a September 23, 1991, *U.S. News and World Report* article titled "America's Beleaguered Bird."

Pages 102–122/Wolf Reintroduction

Barry Lopez's quote is from his *Of Wolves and Men* (Charles Scribner, 1978).

Material concerning Pamela Brown, Carol Martingdale, Sue Larson, Lori Fish (not her real name), and Dan Moore comes from interviews and personal correspondence.

The information on the status of wolves worldwide comes from the article "Endangered Wolf Population Increases" by Jeffrey P. Cohn, in *Bioscience,* vol. 40, no. 9.

Information on reintroduction efforts in behalf of the Mexican wolf can be found in the Endangered Species Reports from 1980 to 1989 issued by the U.S. Fish and Wildlife Service, as well as the 1991 Status Report for Mexican Wolf Recovery Program prepared by David Parsons.

Vanishing Lobo (Johnson Books, 1990), by James C. Burbank, also details the history of reintroduction efforts for the Mexican wolf. The quote from the head of the Mexican wolf recovery team is taken from this book.

Endangered Species Report 19 gives an evaluation of the White Sands Missile Range as a reintroduction site.

Information on North Carolina wolves, as well as wolves in other parts of the United States, can be found in many different articles.

Information on wolf depredation in Minnesota comes from the 1990 U.S. Department of Agriculture report "Wolf Depredation on Livestock in Minnesota." The report also discusses compensation.

The National Park Service provided me with a great deal of information concerning wolves in Yellowstone, including the *Reintroduction and Management of Wolves in Yellowstone National Park and the Central Idaho Wilderness Area: A Report to the United States Congress by the Wolf Management Committee.*

The quote from Thoreau is in *Walden.*

Pages 123–147/Wilderness

The quote by L. David Mech, a noted wolf expert, comes from an interview by Hank L. Fischer in *Defenders of Wildlife Magazine,* vol. 61, no. 6.

The quote by John Muir is in *The American Wilderness in the Words of John Muir* (Country Beautiful, 1973).

The history of wilderness in this country can be found in many sources, including *Land and Resource Planning in the National Forests* (Island Press, 1987) and *Wilderness and the American Mind* (Yale University Press, 1967), by Roderick Nash.

The congressional reports cited are House Committee on Interior and Insular Affairs Reports 95-620 and 95-1821.

The statistics on wilderness were given to me by the Wilderness Society. Part of this section also is based on an interview with Joanne Carter of the Wilderness Society.

The list of wilderness values is from *Philosophy Gone Wild* (Prometheus Books, 1986), by Holmes Rolston III.

Joseph Campbell recounts the story of the chick in his book *The Masks of Gods: Primitive Mythology* (Penguin Books, 1976). The quote by Carl Jung is from his *Psychological Types* (Princeton, 1971).

The connection between our human evolution and our psychic need for wilderness is echoed in *The Long Shore* (Sierra Club Books, 1991), by Jane Hollister Wheelwright. *Wilderness as Sacred Space* (Association of American Geographers, 1991), by Linda H. Graber, is another interesting source.

Statistics on the Gila National Forest were obtained from the Forest Service.

I am indebted to the article "Gardeners in Eden," by Kat Anderson and Gary Paul Nabhan, in the Fall 1991 issue of *Wilderness* for its discussion of early Native American activity in the landscape.

The history of the Gila Wilderness can be found in *The Gila Wilderness* (University of New Mexico Press, 1988), by John A. Murray, as well as many other sources.

I have written earlier of Aldo Leopold for *New Mexico Wildlife* and in the essay "Gila Wilderness" in *Songs of the Fluteplayer: Seasons of Life in the Southwest* (Addison-Wesley, 1991).

Leopold's quote is in *Sand County Almanac*.

Statistics on the Diamond Bar were obtained from the Forest Service.

Most of the information about the Diamond Bar allotment is from Forest Service documents, as well as interviews with Forest Service officials, local environmentalists, and the permittees on the Diamond Bar.

CHAPTER FOUR

Pages 148–157 / Greening of Christianity

The quote by Robert Bellah is from *The Broken Covenant* (Seabury Press, 1975).

Annie Dillard's quote is from *Holy the Firm* (Harper and Row, 1977).

The quote by Lynn White, Jr. is from his article "The Historical Roots of Our Ecologic Crisis," published in the March 10, 1967, issue of *Science*.

The anonymous cowboy poem can be found in *Cowboy Poetry: A Gathering* (Peregrine Smith Books, 1985), edited by Hal Cannon.

"A Cowboy's Prayer," by Badger Clark, is from *Sun, Saddle and Leather* (Gorham Press, 1915).

"Heaven," by Dick Hays, is in his book *From a Cowboy's Point of View* (Dick Hays, Yuma, Arizona, 1992).

The quote by Lynn White, Jr. is from his article "The Historical Roots of Our Ecologic Crisis," published in the March 10, 1967, issue of *Science*.

The reference "an ironic stumbling block" is from Susan Power Bratton's essay in *Religion and Environmental Crisis*, (University of Georgia Press, 1986), edited by Eugene C. Hargrove.

Jay McDaniel's quote is from his essay "Christianity and the Need for New Vision" in *Religion and Environmental Crisis*, (University of Georgia Press, 1986), edited by Eugene C. Hargrove.

The quote by Jay McDaniel concerning animal rights is from *Earth, Sky, Gods and Mortals* (Twenty-third Publications, 1990).

Penelope Washbourn discusses these ideas in her essay "The Dynamics of Female Experience: Process Models and Human Values," in *Feminism and Process Thought* (Edwin Mellen Press, 1981), edited by Sheila Greeve Davaney.

Sallie McFague's quote comes from her essay "Cosmology and Christianity: Implications of the Common Creation Story for Theology," in *Theology at the End of Modernity* (Trinity Press International, 1991), edited by Sheila Greeve Davaney.

John Cobb has written a number of books. He is discussed in *The Rights of Nature: A History of Environmental Ethics* (University of Wisconsin Press, 1989), by Roderick Frazier Nash.

The cover for *Creation Spirituality: Liberating Gifts for the Peoples of the Earth* (Harper San Francisco, 1991), by Matthew Fox was designed by Robert Lentz.

The quote by Matthew Fox that begins "When I speak of original blessings . . . " is from *The Coming of the Cosmic Christ* (Harper and Row, 1988). The remaining quotes by Matthew Fox in this section are also from this book.

The quote by Jay McDaniel is from his essay "Christianity and the Need for New Vision" in *Religion and Environmental Crisis*, (University of Georgia Press, 1986), edited by Eugene C. Hargrove.

Pages 157–168/Native America

The quote by Linda Hogan is from her essay "Walking," in *Sisters of the Earth* (Vintage Books, 1991), edited by Lorraine Anderson.

Statistics on early Native American populations can be found in *The State of Native America* (South End Press, 1992), edited by M. Annette Jaimes, as well as in *American Indian Holocaust and Survival* (University of Oklahoma Press, 1987), by Russell Thorton.

Paula Gunn Allan's quote comes from her essay "IYANI: It Goes This Way," in *The Remembered Earth* (University of New Mexico Press, 1981), edited by Geary Hobson.

The quote by N. Scott Momaday is from an interview with Laura Coltelli in *Winged Words: American Indian Writers Speak* (University of Nebraska Press, 1990), edited by Laura Coltelli.

The quote by Vine Deloria, Jr., is from his *We Talk, You Listen* (Macmillan Company, 1970).

The Portable North American Indian Reader (Viking Press, 1974), edited by Frederick W. Turner III, is one source for a variety of Native American origin tales.

Keith H. Basso's quotes and material come from his book *Western Apache Language and Culture: Essays in Linguistic Anthropology* (University of Arizona Press, 1991).

Two sources for more negative aspects of the Native American's interaction with the land are *Keepers of the Game: Indian-Animal Relationships and the Fur Trade* (University of California Press, 1978), by Calvin Martin, and *Playing God in Yellowstone* (Atlantic Monthly Press, 1987), by Alston Chase.

The quote from Leslie Marmon Silko is from her essay "An Old-Time Indian Attack Conducted in Two Parts," in *The Remembered Earth* (University of New Mexico Press, 1981), edited by Geary Hobson.

The quote by Linda Hogan is from an interview with Laura Coltelli in *Winged Words: American Indian Writers Speak* (University of Nebraska Press, 1990), edited by Laura Coltelli.

The material concerning Tito and Bernice Naranjo is based on interviews and personal correspondence.

Statistics on Native American reservations come from an article in the May 21, 1990, issue of *High Country News*.

The quote by Paula Gunn Allan is from an interview with Laura Coltelli in *Winged Words: American Indian Writers Speak* (University of Nebraska Press,

1990), edited by Laura Coltelli. Paula Gunn Allan's work in this field also can be found in her book *The Sacred Hoop: Recovering the Feminine in American Indian Tradition* (Beacon Press, 1986).

Tito Naranjo's article on the *gia* concept was co-written with his sister Rina Swentzell in 1983.

The High Country News reports regularly on Native American issues and concerns. The quote concerning Huerfano Mountain was from a May 4, 1992, issue; material on the Blackfeet's concern with leasing forest lands for oil and gas exploration was in a May 20, 1991, issue; information on the razing of Hopi shrines was from a January 28, 1991, issue.

More information on cross-cultural conflicts concerning land can be found in material produced by the Southwest Research and Information Center in Albuquerque, notably "The Workbook: The Importance of Cross-cultural Communication between Environmentalists and Land-based People" and "The Workbook: A Struggle for Native Land Rights, the Western Shoshone and the Dann Case."

Pages 169–179/Bioregionalism

The quote by Gary Snyder comes from *The Old Ways* (City Lights Books, 1976).

The material concerning Peter Berg and Judy Goldhaft was obtained through interviews and personal correspondence.

More material on bioregional theater can be found in *Reinhabiting a Separate Country: A Bioregional Anthology of Northern California* (Planet Drum Books, 1978), edited by Peter Berg.

The quote by Gary Snyder on bioregional theater is from his interview titled "Regenerate Culture!" in *Turtle Talk: Voices for a Sustainable Future* (New Society Publishers, 1991), edited by Christopher and Judith Plant.

"Strategies for Reinhabiting Northern California" can be found in *Reinhabiting a Separate Country: A Bioregional Anthology of Northern California* (Planet Drum Books, 1978), edited by Peter Berg.

More information on deep ecology can be found in *Deep Ecology* (Peregrine Smith Books, 1985), by George Sessions and Bill Devall, as well as in *The Rights of Nature: A History of Environmental Ethics* (University of Wisconsin Press, 1989), by Roderick Frazier Nash. George Sessions also has written an article titled "The Deep Ecology Movement: A Review," in the summer 1987 issue of *Environmental Review.*

A Green City Program for San Francisco Bay Area Cities and Towns (Planet Drum Books, 1989) was written and edited by Peter Berg, Beryl Magilavy, and Seth Zuckerman.

More information on the Mattole River Valley can be found in "Living There," by Seth Zuckerman in the March/April 1987 issue of *Sierra*.

Pages 180–193/Jim Corbett

The quote by Frederick Turner comes from his essay "Openings in Religion" in *Rebirth of Value* (State University of New York Press, 1991).

The material concerning Jim Corbett was obtained through interviews and personal correspondence, except where I specifically quote him from *Goatwalking: A Guide to Wildland Living, A Quest for the Peaceable Kingdom* (Viking, 1991).

For more information about Jim Corbett and the Sanctuary movement, see *Convictions of the Heart: Jim Corbett and the Sanctuary Movement* (University of Arizona Press, 1988), by Miriam Davidson.

The essay "The Green Man," by John Fowles, appeared in the autumn 1986 issue of *Antaeus*.

INDEX

Acomas, 166

Africa, environmental problems in, 59, 61, 62, 147

Aldo Leopold Wilderness (New Mexico), 12, 130, 133

Alinsky, Saul, 188

Allen, Paula Gunn, 158, 164

American Indians, 157–169, 187

Animal Damage Control Act, 75

Animal Damage Control (ADC) program, 78–82, 84, 87, 89, 197

biologist for, 90–101

cost of, 92

creation of, 75

Denver Wildlife Research Center, 77, 90–101

statistics on killing of wildlife by, 79–80, 92

wolf and, 123–124

Animals, grazing land needed by, 6, 17–18, 130. *See also* Wildlife; *names of specific animals*

Animal Unit Month (AUM), 17–18, 130

Apaches, 158, 159–161, 168

Arapaho, 158

Audubon Research Center, 70

Bald eagles, 98–99

Basso, Keith, 159–161

Bears, 80, 82–83, 92

Bellah, Robert, 148

Berg, Peter, 169–178

Biologist, 90–101

Bioregionalism, 171–179

Birds

ADC destruction of, 80, 93

bald eagles, 98–99

damage to nesting sites of, 17–18, 28–29

Black bears, 80, 92

Blackfeet, 158, 166, 168

Bobcats, 80, 92

Brock Canyon grazing allotment (New Mexico), 31–33, 35, 40

Brown, Pamela, 102–108, 115, 121

Bureau of Land Management (BLM), 5, 7, 8, 23, 43–45, 86, 126, 138, 196

Camp Creek Exclosure (Oregon), 22

Carson, Rachel, 170
Cather, Willa, 26
Center for Holistic Resource
    Management, 10, 60
Chaney, Ed, 144
Christianity, 149, 152–157, 183,
    187–188
Clark, Badger, 150–151
Cobb, John B., Jr., 154
Coming of the Cosmic Christ, The
    (Fox), 154, 156–157
Communes, 170–171
Connolly, Guy, 90–101
Corbett, Jim, 181–193, 194
Corbett, Pat, 182–187
Corporations, ranching by, 23
Cowboy
    mythology of, 2–3
    poetry of, 149–152
Coyotes, 77, 79, 81, 92, 94, 95–96,
    98
Creation Spirituality: Liberating Gifts
    for the Peoples of the Earth
    (Fox), 154–155

Damage. See Environmental
    damage
Dasmann, Raymond F., 173
Deep ecology, 174, 192–193
Defenders of Wildlife, 77, 83, 84,
    113, 120
Deloria, Vine, Jr., 159
Denver Wildlife Research Center,
    77, 90–101
Desertification, 59
Diamond Bar allotment (New
    Mexico), 133–139, 140, 146
Dillard, Annie, 148

Eagles, 98–99
Ecology
    deep vs. shallow, 174, 192–193
    of ranching, 195–197
El Potrero, 185, 186
Endangered Species Act, 43, 109,
    113, 114, 121
Environmental damage, 4–7, 58–61
    in Africa, 59, 61, 62, 147
    to riparian areas, 5, 21–23,
        28–29, 61, 139
    to wildlife, 17–18, 21, 23,
        28–29, 75–129
Environmental Defense Fund, 114
Environmental groups, 5, 9. See
    also names of specific groups
Environmental Protection Agency,
    78, 174
Erickson, John R., 56
Everglades National Park
    (Florida), 126

Farming, vs. ranching, 189–192
Feller, Joe, 27
Ferguson, Denzel, 15–26, 27, 39,
    64, 70, 71, 72
Ferguson, Nancy, 17–26, 39, 64,
    71, 72
Fish, 21, 23, 177–178
Fish, Jim, 27
Fish, Lori, 111–117, 139–140
Food production, 6, 17–18
Foreman, Dave, 189
Forest and Rangeland Renewable
    Resources Planning Act, 43
Forest Service. See U.S. Forest
    Service
Fowles, John, 193

Fox, Matthew, 154–157
Friends of the Gila River, 28–30,
    33, 37, 41

Ganados del Valle, 36
General Accounting Office
    (GAO), 22, 46, 86, 99
General Land Office, 43
Getty Oil, 23
Gila National Forest (New
    Mexico), 12, 27–41, 125, 127,
    129
Gila Watch, 137
Gila Wilderness (New Mexico),
    12, 132–146
"Goat Cheese Economy of the
    South Baja Sierras, The"
    (Corbett), 182–183
Goats, 180–193
*Goatwalking: A Guide to Wildland
    Living and a Quest for the
    Peaceable Kingdom* (Corbett),
    181
Goldhaft, Judy, 170–179
Good Shepherd Foundation, 80
Government agencies. *See* U.S.
    Bureau of Land
    Management; U.S. Forest
    Service
Grant, Ulysses S., 124
Grazing, amount of land needed
    for, 6, 17–18, 130. *See also*
    Environmental damage;
    Rangeland
Grazing allotments, 5, 7, 8, 9, 23,
    28, 29, 31–33, 35, 40, 86,
    133–139, 140, 146
Grazing violations, 47–52

*Green City Program for San
    Francisco Bay Area Cities and
    Towns, A* (Berg, Magilavy, and
    Zuckerman), 176
Green woman, 193
Grizzly bears, 82–83

Harris, John, 106–107
Hatfield, Connie, 56–60, 63–71,
    72, 96, 144
Hatfield, Doc, 56–60, 63–71, 96
Hays, Dick, 151–152
Hogan, Linda, 157, 161–162
Holistic resource management
    (HRM), 10, 58–64, 67–68
Holistic Resource Management
    (Savory), 67–68
Hopis, 166
Hornocker, Maurice, 81
Humane Society, 92
Hunting, 74–76, 84

Integrated resource management
    (IRM) team, 30–35, 40, 41,
    136, 137
Izaak Walton League, 64–66

Jacobs, Lynn, 27, 189
Johnson, Steve, 27, 76–89, 91, 96,
    97–101
Judeo-Christian tradition, 149,
    152–157, 183, 187–188
Jung, Carl, 161

Kittredge, William, 14

Landscape, response to, 1–2
Larson, Sue, 110–111, 115, 117

Laws
  Animal Damage Control Act, 75
  Endangered Species Act, 43,
     109, 113, 114, 121
  Forest and Rangeland
     Renewable Resources
     Planning Act, 43
  National Environmental
     Protection Act (NEPA),
     29, 43, 101
  National Forest Management
     Act, 43
  Taylor Grazing Act, 44
  Wilderness Act, 125–127
Lee brothers, 74–76, 100–101
Leopold, Aldo, 11, 74, 78,
     132–133, 190
Lessing, Doris, 56
Lions, 74, 75–76, 84, 92, 98, 99
Lopez, Barry, 102
Los Cabreros Andantes, 182
Lummi, 158

MacDonald, Nena, 27–29, 33–41,
     185
MacDonald, Steve, 27–29, 33–41,
     72
Malheur National Wildlife
     Refuge (Oregon), 17–22
Malpais Group, 189
Martingdale, Carol, 110, 115, 116,
     121
Mattole Watershed Salmon
     Support Group, 177–178
McDaniel, Jay, 1, 153, 156
McFague, Sallie, 154
Mech, L. David, 123
Mexican wolf, 102–122

Mexican Wolf Coalition, 111–114
Mexican Wolf Recovery Plan,
     109, 115
Mimbres Valley (New Mexico),
     11–12
Momaday, N. Scott, 158–159
Moore, Dan, 111–117, 121–122,
     129
Mountain lions, 74, 75–76, 84, 92,
     98, 99
Muir, John, 123, 124, 131

Naranjo, Bernice, 167
Naranjo, Tito, 162–169
National Audubon Society, 114
National Environmental
     Protection Act (NEPA), 29,
     43, 101
National Forest Management Act,
     43
National Park Service, 126
National Wilderness Preservation
     System, 125–127
National Wildlife Federation, 5,
     9
Native Americans, 157–169, 187
Native Ecosystems, 27
Natural Resources Defense
     Council, 26
Nature Conservancy, 9, 29, 39
Navajos, 158, 159, 161, 165–166,
     187
New Mexicans Against ADC, 80
New Mexico State University
     Range Improvement Task
     Force, 134
Nez Perce, 159
Nixon, Richard, 78

Oglala, 159
Oman, Don, 42–43, 45–55, 134
Original Blessing (Fox), 154, 155

Papago, 158, 159, 161
Pawnee, 158
Phelps Dodge Mining
    Corporation, 28, 31
Pimas, 160
Plains Indians, 159
Planet Drum Foundation, 174, 176
Poetry, 149–152
Poisoning of wildlife, 77–82, 94,
    97, 99
Pole-planting, 29
Predator Project, 80
Predators, control of, 3, 77–82, 84,
    94–97. *See also names of*
    specific predators
Public lands, 7–11, 14–73
    beef supply and, 72
    costs of grazing on, 23–24
    grazing allotments on, 5, 7, 8, 9,
        23, 28, 29, 31–33, 35, 40,
        86, 133–139, 140, 146
    grazing violations on, 47–52
    holistic resource management
        and, 10, 58–64, 67–68
    subsistence ranching on, 36
Public Lands Action Network, 27
Pueblos, 162–169

Ranchers
    corporations as, 23
    influence of, 19–20
Ranching
    ecology of, 195–197
    economics of, 32

farming vs., 189–192
on public lands. *See* Public lands
Rangeland
    amount of, 3, 5, 7–8, 31–33
    condition of, 4–5
    damage to. *See* Environmental
        damage
    defined, 4
    food production and, 6, 17–18
    See also Grazing allotments;
        Public lands
Rangers, 42–43, 45–55
Rank, Otto, 194
Reagan, Ronald, 78
Redstone grazing allotment (New
    Mexico), 32, 33, 35, 40
Reinhabitation, 169, 173–179
Religious traditions, 149, 152–157,
    183, 187–188
Resource management
    by Forest Service, 43–45
    holistic, 10, 58–64, 67–68
    integrated teams for, 30–35, 40,
        41, 136, 137
Riparian areas, 5, 21–23, 28–29,
    61, 139
Rolston, Holmes, III, 127
Rules for Radicals (Alinsky), 188

Sacred Cows at the Public Trough
    (Ferguson), 15, 19, 26, 27, 64
Saguaro-Juniper Association, 185,
    186, 187, 191
Sanctuary, 184–186
Savory, Allan, 10, 57–63, 67–68,
    121, 147, 192
Sawtooth National Forest (Idaho),
    42, 45–52

Schumacher, E. F., 170
Shaw, Harley G., 90
Sheep, 36, 72, 79, 95, 96, 118
Shoshones, 166
Sierra Club, 9, 27, 114
Silent Spring (Carson), 170
Silko, Leslie Marmon, 161
Sitwell, Edith, 90
Snyder, Gary, 169, 173
Soil erosion, 6, 23
"Strategies for Reinhabiting the
    Northern California
    Bioregion" (Berg), 173
Streams, damage to, 5, 21–23,
    28–29. *See also* Riparian areas
Strickland, Rose, 27
Swentzell, Rina, 168

Taylor Grazing Act, 44
Tewa, 158, 162–169
Thompson, Nick, 160
Tortoises, 85–86
Tourism, 39
Trapping, 79, 80, 84
Trout Creek Mountains Working
    Group, 69–71
Turner, Frederick, 1, 180

Union Oil, 23
United Nations Conference on
    Environment and
    Development, 5
U.S. Bureau of Land Management
    (BLM), 5, 7, 8, 23, 43–45, 86,
    126, 138, 196
U.S. Fish and Wildlife Service,
    109–111, 114, 115, 118, 120,
    126

U.S. Forest Service
    Environmental Assessment
        Report of, 134
    grazing allotments of, 5, 7, 8, 9,
        23, 28, 29, 31–33, 35, 40,
        86, 133–139, 140, 146
    history of, 43–45, 125, 132
    integrated resource
        management teams of,
        30–35, 40, 41, 136, 137
    preservation of wilderness areas
        and, 126, 132–140
    rangers in, 42–43, 45–55
    rights of livestock growers and,
        126
    whistle-blowing in, 50–52, 54
U.S. General Accounting Office
    (GAO), 22, 46, 86, 99
Upper Gila Riparian
    Management Plan, 29–35, 40

Vail Ski Corporation, 23
Varela, Maria, 36
Violence, 18–19

Wald, Johanna, 26, 27
Washbourn, Penelope, 153–154
*Waste of the West: Public Lands
    Ranching* (Jacobs), 27
Water, 6, 22–23, 59. *See also*
    Riparian areas; Streams
Watson grazing allotment (New
    Mexico), 31, 32–33, 35, 40
Watts, Alan, 170
Weber, Kent, 102–108
Welfare ranching, 23–24, 37
*Western Apache Language and
    Culture* (Basso), 159–161

Whistle-blowing, 50–52, 54
White, Lynn, Jr., 148, 152–153, 170
Wilderness Act, 125–127
Wilderness preservation, 125–147
Wilderness Society, 9, 114
Wildlife
    control of predators, 3, 77–82,
        84, 94–97
    damage to, 17–18, 21, 23,
        28–29, 75–129
    hunting of, 74–76, 84
    lethal methods of controlling,
        77–82, 84, 92–94

    nonlethal methods of
        controlling, 79, 93, 96
    statistics on killing of, 79–80, 92
    trapping of, 79, 80, 84
    See also names of specific animals
Wildlife biologist, 90–101
Wildlife Damage Review, 80
Wolf, 102–122
Wolf Action Group, 113
Wolf Management Committee,
    120
Woolf, Virginia, 41
Wuerthner, George, 27